THE ROMANS

ECHOES OF THE ANCIENT WORLD

SERIES EDITOR WERNER FORMAN

THE ROMANS
THEIR GODS AND THEIR BELIEFS

MARGARET LYTTELTON AND WERNER FORMAN

ORBIS · LONDON

For Celia and Francis

© 1984 by Orbis Publishing Limited

First published in Great Britain by
Orbis Publishing Limited, London, 1984.
Reprinted 1985.

Printed in Yugoslavia by Gorenjski Tisk, Kranj
ISBN 0-85613-473-2

CONTENTS

The Changing Image of the City 7

The Traditional Gods of Rome 21

Rites of Sacrifice and Divination 37

Augustus's Religious Revival 61

Private Life and Personal Religion 83

The Mystery Religions 109

Acknowledgments 126
Suggestions for Further Reading 126
Index 126

THE CHANGING IMAGE OF THE CITY

The huge scale and imposing character of the ruins of ancient Rome, many of which still dominate the heart of the modern capital, provide vivid evidence of the power and wealth of the inhabitants of the imperial city. Grandiose monuments decorated with sculpture, such as the Triumphal Arches, the great altars, and the funerary columns of the emperors, bear witness to the skill and sophistication of the ancient Romans, as well as to their prosperity and civic pride. In the towns of Pompeii and Ostia the elegant and spacious residences of the middle and upper classes show plainly the technological skills and high level of material comfort attained by this society.

The remains of ancient Rome played a considerable part in the great artistic and intellectual movement known as the Renaissance. For the suggestive ruins of imperial Rome and the surviving and newly found antique sculptures of the city exercised a profound influence on the development of Western art and architecture from the beginning of the fifteenth century to the start of the nineteenth century, and in some instances beyond. Great artists and architects such as Michelangelo, Mantegna and Palladio derived inspiration from the rediscovery of antiquity. In the eighteenth century the Swiss artist Fuseli depicts himself as overcome by despair at the magnitude of fragments of antique sculpture – in fact the hand and foot from a colossal statue of Constantine. The grandeur of ancient Rome, discerned through the remains of its civilization, and vividly described in Latin literature, also played an important part in the formation of the tastes and sensibilities of writers and their public. Poets like Goethe and Byron were steeped in images of ancient Rome. Edward Gibbon acknowledges in his autobiography the stimulus of the visible remains of the ancient city in determining him to write *The Decline and Fall of the Roman Empire*:

> It was at Rome, on the 15th of October 1764, as I sat musing amidst the ruins of the Capitol, while the bare-footed friars were singing vespers in the Temple of Jupiter, that the idea of writing the decline and fall of the city first started to my mind.

The ancient Romans were supremely practical people; the feats of engineering which we can still see in their buildings, and in their roads, bridges and aqueducts provide ample evidence of this. They also had a genius for organization, revealed in their arrangements for the government of the disparate foreign territories which they gradually acquired and in the

The Aurelian Walls. In the late third century the Emperor Aurelian undertook the construction of the city wall which bears his name in order to defend Rome from attack by barbarians.

7

systematization of the corn supply for Rome, whereby huge supplies of grain were shipped to the city and distributed among the population. Above all, the organization and discipline of the Roman armies reflect these national characteristics. The Romans were not, however, as history textbooks often used to depict them, of an entirely rationalistic cast of mind. On the contrary, the Romans believed that they inhabited a world crowded with a multitude of gods and divine spirits, who had constantly to be invoked or placated in many of the situations of everyday life. In fact the Elder Pliny, writing in the first century AD, asserts in his *Natural History* that the world is populated by a larger number of gods than of mortals. Many of the monuments and buildings of the capital reflect the religious tone of Roman society, and illustrate the importance which Romans attached to the observance of religious rites, and to the worship of their gods. For magnificent temples, some set in extensive precincts, and adorned with countless marble and bronze statues of gods and goddesses, dominated the townscape of ancient Rome.

The religious beliefs and practices of the Romans are worth investigating and evaluating since an understanding of them is fundamental to the comprehension of many aspects of Roman society as a whole. Religion was a powerful force among the Romans, being intertwined with the fabric of society both on the private family level and in the political sphere. The traditional religion underpinned many of the beliefs and mental attitudes of ordinary people, while it gave stability and cohesion to society as a whole.

Many Romans fervently believed that the success and greatness of their city was a reward sent by the gods for their pious observance of the traditional religious rituals. In Rome, religious ceremonies and rites, both public and private, were a prominent feature of daily life. The Romans felt that they were more conscientious than other nations in matters relating to religion. Cicero, the famous orator and politician of the late Republican period, expresses these views clearly in *On the Nature of the Gods* (II, 3,8):

> Rome owes her grandeur and her success to the conduct of those who were tenacious of their religious duties; and if we compare ourselves to our neighbours, we shall find that we are infinitely superior to foreign nations in our zeal for religious ceremonies, although in other respects we may be only equal to them, and in other matters even inferior to them.

Roman religious beliefs and practices are important and interesting not only because they played a fundamental part in the public and private lives of the Romans, but also because to a considerable extent they formed the seed-ground from which Christianity grew up.

From the necessity of imposing some limitations on the vast and complex subject of Roman religious beliefs and rituals, this book is for the most part concerned with the later years of the Republic and the early years of the Empire; that is, approximately the first century BC and the first century AD. These are times of great historical significance and interest, which are relatively well documented in surviving literary and historical writings. Moreover, I have largely concentrated on the religious ceremonies celebrated in the city of Rome, and on the religious practices of the inhabitants of that city and places immediately within her sphere of influence, such as Ostia, the port of Rome. This is for a variety of reasons. Rome as the capital city and heart of a great empire naturally engages our attention. Since Rome was the centre of power we are on the whole better informed about the activities of her citizens than of those of other less important cities. In the period under discussion most of the writers whose accounts of religious observances and beliefs are of supreme importance for the study of Roman religion were born in or lived in Rome.

However, it must be emphasized that there are many gaps in our knowledge of the religious practices and cults of the Romans. This is partly because only very incomplete records and documentation, in the form of inscriptions, have come down to us from antiquity. Our knowledge is largely limited to what ancient writers tell us of religion, although this can be supplemented by archaeological evidence. Hence particular attention is paid in this book to what can be learnt from the remains of temples, shrines and monuments with religious connotations, while the representations of cults and ceremonies on sculpted reliefs and in frescoes, many of which have been recovered in excavations, have been scrutinized for the information they provide on religious rites and cults. In addition, as Roman religion was so deeply conservative and preserved customs and rituals from the remote past, the origins and significance of a considerable number of the ceremonial rites were unknown, or only partially known, to even the educated men of the late Republican and early Imperial periods who have left us accounts of these rituals. Thus in the period we are discussing no one knew in which deity's honour the famous festival of the Lupercalia was celebrated, and although a day was set aside in the Roman calendar for the festival of the goddess Furrina, no one seemed to be able to remember who she was, as Varro, writing in the first century BC complained. Explicit evidence of what the Romans actually believed about their gods, and how they envisioned the divine world, is scarce. For although we may gain some idea of the religious mentality and beliefs of educated Romans, like Varro and Cicero, on the whole we know little of what the ordinary inarticulate members of Roman society felt, beyond what is implied by their participation in religious festivals and rites, both those of the state cults and those celebrated privately in the family.

Overleaf: The Colosseum, Rome. This huge amphitheatre, constructed under the patronage of the emperor Vespasian, has long been a symbol of the power and majesty of Rome. In the interior arena, which was surrounded by tiers of seats providing accommodation for 50,000 spectators, fights between gladiators and between wild beasts and condemned criminals took place.

The richly decorated tomb of the Haterii family, who were perhaps building-constructors, stood three miles outside the city of Rome, beyond the Porta Maggiore. This relief from the tomb shows a number of buildings erected under the Flavian emperors in the first century AD, including the Arch of Titus at the head of the Sacred Way in the Forum, and the arched entrance to the Sanctuary of Isis. The Flavian emperors were devotees of the Egyptian gods.

Above: The she-wolf of Rome, bronze, fifth century BC. Romulus and Remus were added in the Renaissance.

Opposite, below: The sacred geese in front of the Temple of Juno Moneta, Capitoline hill, Rome, second century AD. According to legend, when the Gauls sacked Rome in the fourth century BC, the cackling of these geese gave warning to the Romans of an attempted attack by night on this last point of resistance.

Below: Head of a woman, third century BC, which decorated a tomb in an Etruscan necropolis near Orvieto.

Before going on to discuss the religious beliefs and ceremonies of the Romans, it may be useful to give a brief account of Rome's history and of the development of the city, especially in so far as these impinge upon and relate to Roman religious beliefs. According to the legend, the city of Rome was founded in 753 BC by the twins Romulus and Remus. Owing to the fears of king Amulius, Romulus and Remus were exposed as babies but their lives were preserved by a she-wolf who suckled them; they were rescued by a herdsman, and they grew up to found the city of Rome. Scholars now consider that the Romulus and Remus legend arose considerably after the founding of the city, perhaps some time in the fourth century BC under the influence of similar Greek myths about the founding of cities. According to legend, Romulus founded the city on the Palatine hill, and the so-called hut of Romulus was, according to ancient writers, piously preserved on the Palatine until the fourth century AD. In fact, excavations on the Palatine have revealed traces of Iron Age huts there, some of which appear to date from a century or more before the traditional date for the founding of Rome in 753 BC.

So there was an Iron Age village on the Palatine, very much as tradition recounted, and other settlements grew up on the neighbouring hills in the same period. However, there is little doubt that what gave Rome her initial success and prosperity was the fact that the site lay adjacent to the important bridging point on the River Tiber formed by the Tiber Island. On account of this bridge Rome became an important centre for trade. It has been conjectured that it was because of the importance the bridge had for Rome that the person responsible for the building and up-keep of the bridge was invested with priestly authority; hence, apparently, the original meaning of the word *pontifex* – bridge-maker, which came to be used for priests in general. The old wooden bridge crossed the river at the point where the cattle and vegetable markets known as the *Forum Boarium* and the *Forum Holitorium* grew up. Nearby in the valley between the slopes of the Capitol and Palatine hills, where there had been a cemetery in the Iron Age, the famous Roman Forum was to emerge, after the marshy land had been drained by the building of the *Cloaca Maxima*, or great sewer, probably in the sixth century BC.

With the passing of the centuries, Rome expanded to cover the seven hills in the vicinity of the bridge across the Tiber, and over the valleys between these hills: the Palatine and Capitoline at the centre, the Caelian and Esquiline hills to the east, the Aventine to the south, and the Viminal and Quirinal hills to the north-east. Hence Rome became known as 'the city of the seven hills'. The area comprised by these hills was enclosed by formidable defence walls originally built in the fourth century BC, that is, in the early Republican period.

Our knowledge of the early history of Rome is shadowy and insubstantial, and is very much a matter of dispute among modern scholars. However, it is generally agreed that in the early period Rome was ruled by kings, some of whom were Etruscans, just as tradition relates. The origins of many important Roman institutions can be traced back to this time. The Senate, which came in the ensuing Republican period to play the most powerful and important part in the government of Rome and of its territories overseas, was in origin the council of elders who had advised the kings. With the expulsion of the kings in the late sixth century BC the government was nominally divided between the Senate, consisting first of 300, and later of 600, members, mostly of the wealthy patrician class, and the assemblies of the people, consisting of the poorer classes of citizens. However, the Senate emerged as dominant in this partnership, and came to form the effective government of Rome. The Roman constitution, like the British one, was a product of evolution and custom, rather than a specially designed and written formulation. Roman writers and thinkers, like their later British counterparts, singled out the advantages of such a system. As reported by Cicero, the Elder Cato, the austere moralist and statesman of the second century BC, said:

Our constitution is superior to those of other states because every one of them has been established by a single author of their laws and institutions . . . [it] is based on the genius not of one man but of many; it was established not in one generation but over a period of centuries. For there never lived a man of such great genius that nothing could escape him; nor could the combined powers of all men living at one time possibly make all the necessary provisions for the future, without the aid of actual experience and the test of time.

During the first 500 years or so of the existence of the city of Rome its inhabitants were largely concerned with establishing their ascendancy over Italy south of the River Po. At first they slowly gained control of the territories nearest to the city – Etruria and the Sabine territory to the north, and the Samnite country to the south. The Romans suffered a number of serious setbacks in this period, such as the sacking of the city by a horde of invading Gauls in the early fourth century BC. Early in the third century BC, Rome gained control of the old Greek colonies in southern Italy, after King Pyrrhus of Epirus had given up his attempts to defend them. Within little more than another hundred years the Romans, by a spectacular series of victories, extended their rule over huge territories outside Italy.

Above : Remains of the Pons Aemilius, the oldest stone bridge across the River Tiber, constructed in the second century BC.

By their successes in the three Punic Wars, which were fought in the second half of the third century and the first half of the second century BC, the Romans utterly destroyed Carthage, which had been a formidable maritime power. Thus the Romans freed their city from any serious political threat or commercial rivalry in the western Mediterranean area. By their victories over the Carthaginians the Romans acquired first Sicily and Sardinia, then large areas of Spain, and finally a considerable part of north Africa. The conquered territories were formed into provinces which were governed by those who had served as magistrates. During the second century BC the Romans also conquered the states of Macedonia and Achaia, thus gaining control of Greece. In fact the great cities of Corinth in Greece and Carthage in north Africa were sacked by the Romans in the same year – 146 BC – a date regarded as a significant turning point in the history of Rome. Vast quantities of booty from the wars flowed into the capital – gold, silver, slaves and, from Corinth in particular, Greek works of art. Freed from external dangers and enjoying their increased wealth, the citizens of Rome began to relax their traditionally austere standards of behaviour, and to turn from their martial and thrifty way of life to a luxurious ease. The historian Velleius Paterculus remarked in the first century AD that the sack of Carthage by Scipio Aemilianus had turned the Roman state aside from activity to idleness. The influx of Greek works of art and of other luxury goods had in fact begun earlier with the sack of Syracuse in 212 BC, and some ancient writers considered that the profound changes in the Roman way of life originated in this period; certainly Greek art, and in its wake Greek culture, were deeply to influence the tastes and sensibilities of the Roman upper classes. As the first century BC poet Horace wrote, 'When Greece had been enslaved she made a captive of her rough conqueror, and introduced the arts into rustic Latium.'

Rome continued to gain huge territories overseas; in 133 BC Attalus, the last king of Pergamon, bequeathed his kingdom, which consisted of the rich and well-populated coastal districts of Asia Minor, to Rome. In the following century, Pompey's conquests in the east led to the annexation of Syria, while Julius Caesar's victories in the west led to the annexation of Gaul. However, the power struggles of these great Roman generals in the first century BC, and of their rivals and successors, resulted in an appalling period of strife and civil war, which brought the Roman world to the verge of ruin and plunged it into anarchy. The battle of Actium in 31 BC stands out as another important turning point in Roman history; for in that battle Octavian, later Augustus, decisively defeated Antony and Cleopatra, and by thus firmly establishing his own supremacy throughout the Roman world, brought to an end almost a century of bitter rivalries and civil war. Augustus transformed the government of the state into a *de facto* monarchy, and although he cloaked his real power by preserving the outward forms of Republican government, he in fact inaugurated the rule of the emperors. At a cost to the governing senatorial class of their political power and of their liberty, Augustus restored peace and internal security to the Roman Empire.

Under the rule of succeeding emperors still further territories were added to the already vast Roman Empire; the province of Cappadocia was added in the reign of Tiberius, and the provinces of Mauretania, Britain and Thrace under the emperor Claudius. Following these additions there were few further extensions of the Empire, for its vast frontiers were becoming increasingly difficult to defend against the incursions of Rome's enemies. However, in the reign of Trajan the provinces of Dacia, in what is now Roumania, and that of Arabia, in what is now Jordan and northern Saudi Arabia, were added. During the second century AD the Empire reached its widest extent; there are still impressive remains of Roman rule and occupation to be seen in the widely separated areas which were once part of the Roman Empire.

The acquisition of this vast empire obviously had serious repercussions on the city of Rome itself. The city grew to an immense size, partly as a result of the profits accruing from empire, and partly as a result of the large number of immigrants who came to Rome, either slaves obtained in the conquests overseas, or traders and craftsmen who were attracted by the new commercial opportunities. Estimates made by modern scholars of the population of ancient Rome vary considerably, but it seems likely that there were about a million people living in the city in the first century AD. The philosopher Seneca writing at this time (*Consolation to Helvia*, 6), said, perhaps without exaggerating, that more than half the population of the city consisted of migrants and immigrants, who had flocked to Rome from Italian provincial towns, from colonies overseas, and indeed from all over the world, abandoning their homes and native lands:

Some have been brought by ambition, and some by the necessities of public business, or on diplomatic missions. Others have come to profit from crime and vice, while still others have come as students, or to enjoy the public shows and entertainments. Some have been drawn by friendship, and others by the opportunities to work; some put up for sale their beauty, and others their ability to make speeches – every type of person has flocked to this city which offers high rewards for both virtues and vices.

The rapid increase in the population of Rome was reflected in the character of the streets and buildings of the old residential quarters with their narrow crooked streets and enormous irregular blocks of tenement houses. The tenement houses, which were often poorly constructed of

Opposite, above: The Markets of Trajan, Rome. South-east of the Forum which Trajan had built from the spoils of his Dacian War, he constructed an elaborate market complex on different levels, up the slopes of the Quirinal hill, containing over 150 shops and a large covered hall. They were constructed of Roman concrete, strong mortar combined with lumps of aggregate, and faced with thin red bricks.

Opposite, below: Mummy portrait of a woman on a wood panel. Second or third century AD.

Below: Portrait of an Egyptian, probably third century AD. In Greco-Roman Egypt, such portraits were apparently kept at home during the subject's lifetime, and added on his death to his mummified corpse.

15

Left : The Baths of Caracalla, built in Rome in the early third century AD. The construction of this huge, vaulted complex of bath buildings was made possible by the use of Roman concrete. The bath buildings were embellished with mosaic floors and architectural features, such as elaborate capitals carved in marble.

Left : Street in Ostia, the harbour town of Rome. Something of the character of the 'new town' of Rome, built after the fire of AD 64, can be appreciated in the surviving streets of Ostia. The new buildings of Rome were similar to those which can still be seen at Ostia, being constructed of concrete faced with regular brickwork which formed a utilitarian and functional style of architecture.

The Aurelian Walls of Rome (see page 6). These walls still survive for much of their original length of twelve miles. They present an imposing appearance, pierced by eighteen towered gateways, and strengthened by more than 300 square towers.

half-timbered work, mud brick, and wattle and daub, were built to reckless heights; although seventy feet was imposed as the legal limit for the height of such buildings under Augustus, many older houses no doubt exceeded this. Great fires, collapsing houses, and floods caused by the River Tiber were a constant danger to the inhabitants. The crowded streets of the old city were teeming with life and activity, for there were shops, or *tabernae*, and workshops along the façades of the tenement blocks; in Rome there was no separation between the residential and bazaar quarters of the town, such as exists in the towns of the Orient. Craftsmen of the same trade and shops selling the same wares were often grouped together along a single street, as was the case in medieval towns, and is even today in some quarters of an old-fashioned place like Istanbul.

Day and night ancient Rome was a noisy place, as impecunious poets, forced to live in cheap lodgings, complained. Martial (*c.* AD 40–*c.* 104) inveighed against the early-rising bakers, the day-long banging of the coppersmith's hammers, and the constant rattle of the money-changers at work, while the satirist Juvenal railed against the loud rumble of the carts through the narrow streets at night, and the shouts of men herding cattle and other animals through the city. Seneca, who at one time lived very close to a public bath, in one of his *Letters* (LVI) describes the sounds that

17

assailed him – the grunts of the exercising athletes, the shouts and splashes from those plunging into the water, and continues:

> Imagine the hair-plucker, with his penetrating, shrill voice – for purposes of advertisement – continually shouting, and never holding his tongue except when he is plucking someone's armpits and making his victim yell instead. Then the cake-seller with his varied cries, the sausageman, the sweet-maker, and all the vendors of food hawking their wares, each with his distinctive cry.

A decisive change in the construction and appearance of the town took place after the great fire of Rome in AD 64. It raged for six days, severely damaging ten of Rome's fourteen districts. The opportunity to construct a new city after the destruction of so much of the old one was eagerly and intelligently seized by the emperor Nero. A new town with broad streets and spacious buildings of restricted height and regular dimensions and alignment was created.

In the vast expansion of the city, buildings had already by the first century BC spread beyond the circuit of the Republican Walls. It was not until the end of the third century AD that Rome was again enclosed by defensive walls. These walls, known as the Aurelian Walls after the emperor Aurelian during whose reign they were built, encompass an area so huge that it easily contained the population of the modern city of Rome until the last years of the nineteenth century. As late as 1870, much of the land within the ancient walls of the city had still not been built over; a photograph taken around 1870 shows the great Lateran Basilica surrounded by fields and vineyards. During late antiquity and the Middle Ages the population of ancient Rome had decreased to such an extent that the greater part of the area covered by the ancient city was more or less abandoned, and reverted to being farming land or even wasteland, with only a few scattered houses. In medieval times the centre of the city shifted north of the Capitoline hill to the district within the great bend in the River Tiber where the Pantheon stands, and to the area across the river known as Trastevere, in the vicinity of St Peter's. What had once been the centre of ancient Rome became deserted and overgrown with vegetation. The ruins of the Roman Forum and the ridge and slopes of the Palatine hill, where the palaces of the emperors had stood, were covered with vineyards, trees and fields, while ramshackle houses invaded the ruins of the buildings at the foot of the Capitoline hill. Even in the seventeenth century, as drawings and paintings show, cattle were grazing in the Forum; in fact the Forum became known as 'Campo Vaccino', or field of cows. Thus the magnificent centre of Imperial Rome sank back into something approaching what had been its primeval state, before the founding of the city. That scene had been vividly conjured up by poets of the Augustan period; as Tibullus wrote, 'When Romulus had not yet built the fortification walls of the eternal city, then cows were pastured on the grassy Palatine, and poor cottages stood on the hill where there is now the temple of Capitoline Jupiter'. (Tibullus, II, v, 23–6.) Many hundred years later the wheel was to come almost full circle.

The Stadium of Domitian, part of the imperial palace on the Palatine hill. The vast and imposing palace was largely constructed under the Flavian emperors. To the south-east of the palace buildings are the remains of a long walled garden, which was laid out in the form of a stadium.

THE TRADITIONAL GODS OF ROME

We are not accustomed to think of the Romans as a particularly religious people. By contrast with other societies of the ancient world, such as the hieratically organized society of Egypt, or the theocratic state of the Jews, the Romans seem to have been remarkably secular, and even modern, in their outlook on the world. After all, in, say, the first century BC Roman society was a relatively open one, in which even recently freed slaves might make good, acquiring wealth and a certain social position, where women were not kept in seclusion and where a career in the army might enable men of the poorer classes to acquire land of their own.

Of course the Romans had a traditional religion, with a plethora of gods, rites and ceremonies, but some of the more articulate members of society seem to have regarded these with scepticism. During the First Punic War one of the consuls, Publius Claudius Pulcher, on hearing that the sacred chickens would not eat, as this was regarded as a bad omen, drowned them; 'If they will not eat, let them drink', he said, and flung them into the sea. Cicero, although he always expressed the deepest respect for the religion in his speeches in the law courts, seems to have harboured serious doubts about its validity. These come out in his philosophical writings. In his dialogue *On the Nature of the Gods* he has one of the speakers set out numerous arguments against the existence of the gods, while in his book *On Divination* he seriously questions belief in omens, prodigies, prophetic dreams and astrology. Indeed, much later, St Augustine was to comment that Cicero would never have dared to say in public what he wrote in private.

In the first century BC the poet Lucretius was perhaps the most impassioned sceptic of all the Romans. In *On the Nature of Things* (V, 1198 ff.) he eloquently mocked what he regarded as the superstitious man:

> . . . seen often with veiled head turning towards a stone, approaching every altar, or lying prostrate on the ground and stretching out one's hands before the shrines of the gods, sprinkling the altars with the streaming blood of animals and linking vow with vow.

In 79 AD the down-to-earth emperor Vespasian, mocking the fact that the Romans posthumously deified their emperors, remarked sadly as he lay dying, 'Alas, I think I am becoming a god' (Suetonius, *Life of Vespasian*, XXIII).

Yet in judging the strength of religion in Roman society it is best not to be unduly influenced by the scepticism of a relatively small number of prominent and highly educated individuals. There undoubtedly was a current of rationalism in the thinking of the upper classes of the late Republic, but this tendency was never taken to its logical conclusion, that is, the total rejection of religious practices and beliefs. Although these

Marble statue of Aphrodite. A copy of a celebrated Hellenistic statue of the third century BC. The Romans assimilated Venus with the Greek goddess of love, Aphrodite.

Opposite: The Temple of Vesta, the Forum,
Rome, sacred to the cult of Vesta, goddess of
the hearth. In this shrine, the sacred fire was
kept constantly burning, tended by the Vestal
Virgins. The ancient shrine was many times
rebuilt; the present remains date largely from
the early third century AD.

*Below: Fresco showing Hercules and a
worshipper. Hercules is identifiable by his club.
This painting comes from a tomb in one of the
cemeteries near Ostia. Hercules is a popular
subject for portrayal in the tombs of the
inhabitants of Ostia, perhaps reflecting the local
importance of his cult. He was often regarded as
patron of the dead because he was believed to
have rescued Alcestis from the underworld.*

religious traditions were eventually discredited and abandoned in favour
of the doctrines of Christianity, their ultimate failure should not blind us to
the fact that for more than a thousand years the Romans kept up these
religious observances; these were the beliefs which sustained them, and
which regulated a considerable part of their lives.

The Roman concept of religion requires an acceptance of a number of
attitudes unfamiliar to us which were deeply rooted in the minds of the
Romans. The fact that there were close connections between religion and
politics in ancient Rome has sometimes been taken by modern scholars to
show that Roman religion was hollow and insincere, or in the grip of decay.
For example, the meetings of electoral assemblies of the Roman people
could only be held if no unfavourable omens were observed either before-
hand or during the proceedings. Meetings of the Senate might also be
suspended, or its decisions influenced by the observance of unfavourable
signs or omens. Undoubtedly the observance of signs and omens was
sometimes exploited by political factions to their own advantage, but
scholars now suggest that the degree of political trickery and chicanery
has been exaggerated. It is argued that it was only a very narrow Christian-
izing approach that allowed scholars to deduce decline or decay in the
religion of Rome from its close involvement with political decisions and
procedures. It is now realized that 'the range of mundane ends for which
religion is conceived to be instrumental is as broad as the range of all human
ends' (Spiro, in *Anthropological Approaches to the Study of Religion*, 106).

The widespread acceptance of traditional religious beliefs throughout a
large part of the Roman Empire was important in giving cohesion and
stability to Roman society. The unity of a complex political system, such as
that of the Roman Empire, depends not just on shared institutions, such as
a common system of law and of military defences, but also on shared beliefs
and symbols in the minds of the people. These were to a considerable
extent supplied by traditional religion.

In Rome there were close links between religion and society; the links
between the state cults and the governing class were particularly strong.
There was no separate priestly class: all the priests were elected or co-opted
from members of the governing class in the Republican period, and they
often performed the two functions simultaneously. For example Julius
Caesar was both consul and *pontifex maximus* (chief priest) in 44 BC. Those
elected as priests were simply prominent citizens, and were ordinary
laymen, not professional experts in religious affairs.

In the late Republic and early Empire there were four important colleges
of priests: sixteen *pontifices*, sixteen augurs, fifteen men (*Quindecimviri*) for
the overseeing of foreign cults, and a College of Epulones, or feast
organizers. These last organized the banquet for senators after the festival
of Jupiter on the Capitol, and public banquets held after other festivals and
games.

Under the Monarchy the king had been the chief priest of the state, but
with the establishment of the Republic the king's ceremonial and religious
duties were transferred to a high priest, known as *pontifex maximus*, who
was elected by a special assembly of the people. His official residence was
the *Regia*, formerly the palace, in the Forum. In Imperial times this office
was held by the reigning emperor. The *pontifex maximus* presided over the
college of *pontifices* which formed the supreme college of priests. Their
name suggests that they were in origin connected with the magic rites of
bridge-building, as previously described, but they evolved into an advisory
body on religious affairs with overall responsibility for the conduct of
religious rites and rituals. They controlled the religious calendar and
arranged the holy days and intercalary months. Julius Caesar as *pontifex
maximus* was able to introduce his reforms to the calendar which has
remained almost unchanged down to the present time. However, it was
often the magistrates of the Roman state, rather than the priests, who
played the chief parts in the leading sacrifices and rituals of the state cults.

The second most important college of priests was that of the augurs, who

View of the Piazzale delle Corporazioni from the reconstructed theatre, Ostia. This square, with a small temple in the middle, and surrounded by colonnades, was an important centre of commerce, for around it were the offices of the local merchants and shipwrights, and of their overseas clients. The temple in the middle may have been maintained by one of the trade guilds.

by means of divination from the flight and calls of birds decided whether certain proposed actions had the approval of the gods. The augurs did not go beyond this; they were not expected to be able to foretell the future. It was a coveted honour to be elected to either of these colleges of priests. Cicero, in spite of his scepticism, was delighted to be elected an augur. The *Quindecimviri*, or Board of Fifteen, were chiefly responsible for the care and interpretation of the Sibylline Books. They acquired a general oversight of the non-Latin cults, such as that of Cybele, which had been imported to Rome. The historian Tacitus was a member of the board.

To a considerable extent the ordinary Roman was relieved from the religious duty of propitiating the gods by the institution of the state cults, which were maintained by the priests and elected magistrates. It was believed that by means of these cults the right relationship or *pax deorum*, 'peace of the gods', between the state and the gods was maintained. This was thought essential for the success and prosperity of the Roman state. Romans believed the 'peace of the gods' could be maintained by prayers and sacrifices carried out according to time-honoured rituals, and by means of divination to ensure that omens were favourable to any pre-meditated enterprise, such as a military campaign, or the founding of a new city. It was part of any magistrate's or official's duties to carry out the appropriate religious ceremonies, under the supervision of the relevant priests, before undertaking important governmental duties. Magistrates were required to hold religious ceremonies on entering office, and before setting out on a campaign, or holding a census, or summoning an important meeting.

The Romans worshipped a large number of gods of quite markedly different kinds and of different origins. They ranged from great divinities such as Jupiter and Juno, and deified heroes like Hercules, with whom the state cults were largely concerned, to spirits of the countryside, and within the family the household gods and spirits of dead ancestors. This was for a number of reasons; partly it reflected the Roman cast of mind, and partly the long historical evolution through which the city passed. Roman religion came to embrace not just a few, but many religious cults which were adopted from other peoples with whom the Romans came into contact or conflict. The adoption of alien cults, particularly in early times, was often seen as a means of overcoming an enemy people, by importing their chief deity to Rome. Indeed, according to tradition the Romans were unable to defeat the neighbouring Etruscan city of Veii until they had by a special prayer induced the goddess Juno to abandon Veii, and had enticed her to migrate to Rome.

Edward Gibbon, in *Decline and Fall of the Roman Empire* (vol. I, ch. II), elegantly describes the mental attitudes of the ancient Roman polytheist and his inclination towards religious syncretism:

> Fear, gratitude, and curiosity, a dream or an omen, a singular disorder or a distant journey, perpetually disposed him to multiply the articles of his belief, and to enlarge the list of his protectors. . . . The deities of a thousand groves and a thousand streams possessed, in peace, their local and respective influence; nor could the Roman who deprecated the wrath of the Tiber, deride the Egyptian who presented his offering to the beneficent genius of the Nile. The visible powers of nature, the planets, and the elements, were the same throughout the universe. The invisible governors of the moral world were inevitably cast in a similar mould of fiction and allegory. . . . Such was the mild spirit of antiquity, that the nations were less attentive to the difference, than to the resemblance, of their religious worship.

The character of Roman religion was much affected by the fact that the Romans were not creative thinkers by temperament, and did not ask fundamental questions about the processes of nature. Unlike the Greeks, they did not produce philosophers or scientists who attempted to provide scientific explanations for natural phenomena, and for the origin of the world. Even highly educated Romans had no secure basis for a scientific and rational view of the world, and the way was left open for the inclusion, or intrusion, of supernatural powers. The sense of human helplessness and vulnerability in the face of the vastness of the universe and the feeling of anxiety and fear when confronted by unpredictable occurrences form an important part of the foundations of Roman religion – as of all religions. In fact most Romans seem to have regarded all important natural processes, such as the enjoyment of good health and the growth of the crops, as being under the control of different gods, and even the prosperity of the state and

The ships and the great harbour of Claudius, with its tall lighthouse, were essential to Ostia's trade. They are represented on several mosaics of the city and its cemeteries. This mosaic comes from the Isola Sacra necropolis, which was the cemetery of those who lived in the settlements round the harbours known as Portus.

that of the individual, were thought of as divinely activated. The chief function of Roman religion on both a public and a private level was the propitiation of the relevant gods so as to ensure success in all matters involving the state and the individual. Roman religion was essentially concerned with prosperity and with success. 'Jupiter is called Best and Greatest,' wrote Cicero, 'not because he makes us just or sober or wise, but because he makes us healthy, rich and prosperous' (*On the Nature of the Gods*, III, 36).

The Romans were in origin an agricultural people, and some of their oldest gods were those who presided over agricultural processes and aspects of farming life, such as Flora, goddess of flowers, Pomona, goddess of fruit, Ceres, goddess of creation and growth, Robigus, the god who averted blight, and Vesta, goddess of the hearth. The cult of Vesta, which was possibly Greek in origin, remained of great importance throughout Rome's long history. In addition to the private cult of Vesta practised by individual families there was also a state cult of this goddess. The chief shrine of Vesta was a small round temple in the Roman Forum, which according to tradition had been founded by Numa Pompilius, the second king of Rome. The circular form of this temple may reproduce that of the huts of the early inhabitants of Rome. Certainly ancient authors believed that its round shape, which was unusual for a temple, was inherited from the remote period of the kings; as the poet Ovid (43 BC–AD 17) writes, 'The building which you now see roofed with bronze, you might then have seen roofed with thatch, and the walls woven of tough oziers' (*Fasti*, VI, 261).

In this shrine the sacred fire was kept constantly burning, and was rekindled only once a year by the Vestal Virgins. It is generally thought that the origin of the state cult of Vesta is to be found in the hearth cult of the ancient royal household of Rome, going back to a time when fire was so precious that one flame was always kept burning in the community. It is suggested that the Vestal Virgins were originally the daughters of the kings. The Vestal Virgins played an important part in many of the festivals celebrated annually in Rome, and they prepared and stored a number of special substances used in the various religious rituals such as the sacrificial cake (*mola salsa*).

There were six Vestals, who were elected as children to serve for thirty years, after which they might retire and marry. Apparently few did so, for there was a tradition of bad luck associated with such marriages. Great stress was laid on the virginity of those who became Vestal Virgins and on their total abstinence from sexual intercourse during their term of service. For in antiquity sexual intercourse was believed to be polluting, and to debar a person from close contact with a deity. Burial alive was the fate which awaited Vestals who failed to remain chaste. During the period of their office, they lived in the House of the Vestal Virgins, adjacent to the temple. The Vestals came under the jurisdiction of the *pontifex maximus*.

Another god whose cult was of great antiquity was the two-faced Janus, a spirit of the door of the house, and of gateways (the Latin word *ianua* means door). Consequently Janus came to be regarded as the god of beginnings, and January, the first month of the revised calendar, is named after him. In Rome he was worshipped in, among other places, the Regia in the Roman Forum. As the Regia was in early times the palace of the kings of Rome, Janus's rites may originally have been connected with the king's door.

Jupiter the sky-god, who was believed to cause storms and bring rain, as well as controlling the daylight, was another ancient god. To an agricultural people, he was obviously of great importance. As he was thought to cause thunder he was often represented with a thunderbolt in one hand. In origin Jupiter was probably connected with the great sky-gods of the near east, such as Ahura-Mazda in Iran, Baal in Syria, and possibly Yahweh, god of the Hebrews. The chief temple of Jupiter, that on the Capitoline hill in Rome, was, according to tradition, founded by the last kings of Rome, and dedicated in 509 BC, the first year of the Republic.

So-called Temple of Venus, at Hadrian's Villa, Tivoli. A copy of the famous Temple of Aphrodite at Cnidos in Asia Minor, which reputedly housed the first nude cult statue of the goddess.

House of the Vestal Virgins, the Forum, Rome. The six Vestals lived in this building throughout the period of their office. The form of their original house is not known, but after the fire of AD 64 a spacious residence was constructed for them, set around a long colonnaded court. Statues of the Vestals decorate the court.

28

Jupiter Optimus Maximus – the Greatest and the Best – soon came to be regarded as the patron god of the Roman state. He was associated in this temple with Juno, his consort, and Minerva, the craft goddess, forming a triad. Consequently this temple had three *cellae*, or shrines in the interior, one for each of these deities.

As Rome's interests and influence grew, and as her power expanded, new gods were added to those which the old farming community had worshipped. Owing to Rome's increasing contact with the Greeks, other Greek deities were added to those already worshipped at Rome. The cultural history of Rome is to a considerable extent the history of her transformation through contact with Greek ideas. At first this took place largely through her connections with the Etruscans, who down to the end of the seventh century BC ruled over Rome itself. However, Rome appears also to have been in direct contact with the Greeks from early times.

When the Roman general Camillus conquered the Etruscan town of Veii, just to the north of Rome, in 384 BC – this was the time when the power of the Etruscans was waning – he dedicated a bronze bowl to the Greek god Apollo at Delphi. Already in the fifth century BC a temple to Apollo had been established in Rome, probably as a result of a plague in the city, as Apollo was regarded as the god of healing. Apollo was also associated with the sun, and Augustus built a magnificent temple to him on the Palatine hill, which was crowned by a golden chariot containing Apollo as the sun-god.

According to the tradition recounted by Livy, the twin gods Castor and Pollux, originally heroes, known as the Dioscuri, were adopted by the Romans from the Greeks in 484 BC, as a result of their fighting on the Roman side at the battle of Regillus. They then appeared miraculously at Rome on horseback by the Fountain of Juturna in the Roman Forum to bring news of the victory over the Etruscans. So it came about in Rome that they were particularly associated with the cavalry, and a ceremonial cavalry parade was part of the festival celebrated in their honour.

Among the Greeks, however, both those of the mainland and those of Sicily, the cult of the Dioscuri was particularly associated with navigation, and this aspect of their cult was observed at Ostia, the port of Rome, where an important festival was held in their honour. As late as the mid-fourth century AD it was believed that Castor and Pollux could procure good weather for ships. The historian Ammianus Marcellinus (XIX, 10, 4 in R. Meiggs, *Ostia*, 345) recounts that in 359 AD storms prevented ships with grain sailing into the harbour at Ostia, and there was a danger of food riots in Rome. Then:

> While Tertullus [the prefect of the city] sacrificed in the Temple of the Castors, the wind dropped and the sea was calmed; then the winds turned to a gentle breeze from the south, and the ships in full sail entered the harbour, and filled the granaries with corn.

The Greek hero Heracles was also adopted by the Romans at an early date, under the name Hercules. His most ancient place of worship in Rome was at an altar in the *Forum Boarium*, the old market-place of the city. His cult was especially popular with merchants, perhaps because he was believed to be able to ward off dangers on the long journeys which merchants had to undertake.

In addition to taking over the worship of some of the Greek gods and demi-gods, or heroes, like Heracles, in many instances the traditional gods of Rome came to be assimilated by the Romans with their Greek equivalents. For example Jupiter, the sky-god, and Juno, his consort, came to be assimilated with the Greek sky-god Zeus and his wife Hera. Minerva the Italian handicraft goddess was early on identified by the Romans with the Greek goddess Athena, and the Italian goddess Venus came to be equated with the Greek goddess of love, Aphrodite. Venus was claimed as an ancestor by Julius Caesar, who dedicated a temple to her in Rome. She

29

Right : Temple at the north end of the Forum at Ostia. Built on an unusually high podium so as to dominate its surroundings, this was probably the Capitolium, or temple dedicated to the Capitoline triad of Jupiter, Juno and Minerva. A temple dedicated to this triad came to be a prominent feature of many Roman towns, both in Italy and overseas.

Above : First century BC head of a marble statue of Zeus, copied from a Greek bronze original of about 450 BC. The Romans assimilated Zeus, chief of the Greek gods, with Jupiter.

Opposite, left : Decorative terracotta plaque from the Temple of Apollo on the Palatine showing Apollo and his sister Artemis (Diana) decorating a sacred pillar. The Neo-Attic style of these reliefs reflects Augustus's classicizing taste.

Opposite, below right : Decorative terracotta relief from the Temple of Apollo on the Palatine. This detail of the plaque shows Apollo disputing possession of the Delphic tripod with Hercules – Hercules stands on the other side of the tripod. This temple was dedicated to Apollo by Augustus in 28 BC. Augustus believed himself to be under Apollo's protection, and attributed his victory at Actium to the god's intervention.

also acquired considerable mythological significance among educated Romans as the legend grew up that she was the mother of Aeneas, the Trojan prince who had escaped from the Greeks at the sack of Troy and had come to Italy to make possible the eventual founding of the Roman state; this legend was immortalized by Virgil, the great epic poet of the first century BC, in the *Aeneid*. Similarly Mars, the Italian god of war in whose honour impressive games and festivals were held, as his cult was obviously important to the warlike Roman people, came to be associated mythologically with Ares, the Greek god of war.

All these Greek gods, who were known as the Olympians as they were believed to dwell on Mount Olympus when they were not engaged in intervening (or meddling) in human affairs, were much less shadowy figures than the gods of Rome with whom they came to be associated. The Greek Olympians were not impersonal figures, but rather a family whose passions, experiences, and even weaknesses were conceived of as very similar to those of the human beings over whom they presided. The stories of their lives were celebrated in Greek art and poetry. The Romans, by assimilating their gods with those of the Greeks, gradually acquired from oral tradition, from literature, and from representations in sculpture and paintings, a rich mythology. These myths came to colour much of the Romans' own art and literature, and to a lesser extent their ways of thinking about the gods. However, in the actual practice of Roman religion, as opposed to accounts of the activities of the gods in Greek-influenced literature, the personalities of the gods were of little consequence; in the rituals of the state cults the people paid their respects to the gods in a formal way and on an impersonal basis.

In fact a number of educated and articulate Romans questioned the often scurrilous accounts of the deeds of the gods given by the poets; these accounts they called 'the religion of the poets'. Mucius Scaevola, *pontifex maximus* in the early first century BC, was recorded as saying that religion could be divided into three types – the religion of the poets, the religion of the state, and the religion of the philosophers, and he dismissed the religion of the poets as mere invention. In his dialogue *On the Nature of the Gods* (I, 16) Cicero has one of the speakers echo this view:

> Not much less ridiculous than the opinions – or rather the ravings – of the philosophers are the outpourings of the poets who have represented the gods as enraged with anger and inflamed with lust; who have brought before our eyes their wars, fights, battles and wounds; and in addition their hatreds, quarrels, births and deaths; their indulgence in every kind of excess, their passions, their adulteries, their love affairs with mortals.

To a limited extent the Romans also worshipped abstract deities; a Temple of Concord was dedicated in the fourth century BC, and the remains of the Augustan restoration of this temple can still be seen in the

Roman Forum. Shrines or altars were set up to *Honos* (military honour), to *Virtus* (courage), *Pietas* (piety) and *Pudicitia* (conventional sexual conduct). At the shrines of *Pudicitia* the sacrifices had to be offered by women who had been married only once; not surprisingly perhaps, the cult seems to have died out by the late Republican period.

In addition to all the gods known by name, the Romans worshipped a number of rather vague divine powers or spirits, sometimes called *numina*. The everyday world of the Romans was populated by a multitude of divine spirits, envisaged more or less as intermediate between men and the powerful gods of heaven and the underworld. It is easy to underestimate the importance of the supernatural world in the thoughts and apprehensions of the Romans; their lives were overshadowed by the apparently inexplicable elements in the world around them. These they tried constantly to control by prayers, sacrifices and even magic. For the Romans believed that religious words and formulae had power. In his *Natural History* (XXVIII, 3) the Elder Pliny writes:

> Do magic words and spells have any power? . . . individually, one by one the wisest have no faith in such things; but collectively throughout their everyday lives, they act as though they believe, without being aware of it.

The Romans believed that much of the countryside was inhabited by spirits. Groves, woods, caves, streams and springs were often considered sacred on account of being the dwelling places of these shadowy figures, of which not even the sex was usually known. Latin poets celebrate these spirits. Ovid writes about one of the hills of Rome, describing it as it was in early times – 'There was a grove below the Aventine dark with the shade of holm-oaks, and when you saw it you would say, "There is a deity there."' In his famous 'Ode to the spring of Bandusia' Horace makes clear that he regards it as sacred: 'O spring of Bandusia, more brilliant than glass, deserving a libation of sweet wine accompanied by flowers, to-morrow I'll make you a gift of a kid.' (*Odes* III, 13, 1). The Elder Pliny writes that trees were believed to be the dwelling places of spirits, and that according to an ancient ritual, simple farming communities even in his day sometimes dedicated a conspicuous tree to a god. 'We worship groves, and their very silences,' he says.

Many of the large rivers of Italy were honoured by cults, especially the River Tiber, which was often represented as a bearded old man. Crossroads also, both those in towns and the countryside, were thought of as presided over by spirits, the *Lares compitales*, which were propitiated in local festivals provided by district leaders.

In traditional Roman religion the supremely important thing was the conscientious and correct performance of time-honoured rituals and prayers. If a mistake was made, it was regarded as essential to repeat the whole rite. The historian Livy reports more than one occasion when the

Above: Temple of Castor and Pollux, the Forum, Rome. The original temple was consecrated in 484 BC. These three surviving columns, which are of Carrara marble, date from the rebuilding of the temple carried out by the emperor Tiberius between 7 BC and AD 6.

elaborate Latin Festival, which the Latin cities celebrated on Mount Albano, had to be repeated from the very beginning on account of an error. Throughout much of Rome's history, at any rate down to the end of the first century BC, it was not thought that the chances of conciliating the gods depended on the good character of the worshipper; what really mattered was the correct performance of the right rituals. Hence, there was in the traditional religion of Rome a very considerable split between religion and morality as we think of it. This is to us an extraordinary state of affairs, and indeed this attitude towards religion among the Romans was considerably modified in the first two centuries AD as the result, on the one hand, of the influence of schools of philosophy, such as Stoicism, and on the other, owing to the introduction into the Roman Empire of various oriental religions.

Although the Romans were almost obsessively convinced of the need to propitiate the gods by sacrifices and prayers, their religious beliefs appear to have had relatively little effect on their day-to-day conduct. Anticipation of divine retribution only rarely seems to have affected their behaviour; fears of hell did not loom anything like so large in the minds of the Romans as among the Greeks before them, or the Christians after them. Nevertheless morality was a powerful force among the Romans; it was simply that for the most part the Romans did not deduce their morals from the nature of their gods. The contrast with Christianity is very great in this respect. The Romans had no equivalent of the Bible, with its code of the Ten Commandments, and its numerous other moral injunctions about behaviour. However, much of Roman literature, in particular their historical writing, is heavily moralizing, inculcating the martial virtues of honour, courage, and above all patriotism, which were appropriate to this military society. As Horace wrote: 'It is pleasing and honourable to die for the fatherland' (*Odes* III, 2, 13). The moral code of the Romans was chiefly supported by family traditions and concern for public esteem and reputation. Family pride was all important; in an upper-class household the children grew up surrounded by the death masks or portraits of their ancestors, inscribed with their deeds and their honours. The *dignitas*, or honour, and rank of the family, and of the individual, were jealously

Opposite : Stucco decoration from the ceilings of a house beneath the Villa Farnesina, Rome, dating from the late first century BC. These attractive representations of landscape show several examples of sacred trees incorporated in simple shrines. Right : A winged Victory also forms part of the decoration of this house.

Left : Marble relief of Republican date found near the Temple of Hercules at Ostia. The scene on the right appears to show an archaic Greek statue of Heracles (Hercules) being dredged up from the sea in a fishing net, suggesting that the cult statue of this temple was a Greek original brought to Italy and rescued from a shipwreck. In the central scene Hercules hands a tablet with an oracle to a boy, while a third scene perhaps relates to the interpretation of this oracle by a soothsayer. So the cult of Hercules at Ostia appears to have provided oracles.

33

guarded and zealously promoted. In this self-aggrandizing society the highest mark of public esteem a man could receive was the award of Triumph; surrounded by captives and the spoils of war, he rode in chariot to the Capitol wearing the robes and crown of Jupiter.

Much of Roman moralizing has a secular and pragmatic tone; in play and poems impressionable young men are urged not to waste an inheritance and so come to a bad end like so-and-so's son, or to indulge in unseemly affairs with prostitutes or promiscuous married women, and so get a bad reputation. There was, however, an important although circumscribed area of morality where the sanctions were provided by religious beliefs. For some offences the Romans believed were punishable by the gods. Socially the most significant of these offences was the breaking of an oath (*fides*), or other form of agreement, such as the ties between the patron and his clients. Rich and influential Romans acquired a huge *clientela*, or following of dependents such as freed slaves, poorer relations, aspiring writers, and even soldiers from armies they had commanded. Patron and clients were bound together by an obligation to help each other, the breach of which was regarded as no less serious than the breaking of an oath, and similarly punishable by the gods. Much depended on the maintenance of this relationship of mutual trust between a patron and his clients; these clients the patron defended in the law courts, and assisted with gifts, and even meals, in return for their loyal support. The size of a man's following in the Forum, or at the baths, or at the games, might boost his social and political standing.

The Romans believed that perjury would be punished by the god in

whose name the oath had been sworn. The belief in the sanctity of oaths was of practical utility; when an army camp was established the military tribunes administered an oath to all its occupants that they would steal nothing, and the soldiers took oaths that the booty and spoils of war would be fairly distributed. Polybius, a Greek who spent some time in Rome in the second century BC, attributed to their belief in the sanctity of oaths the Romans' relative scrupulousness in the handling of public money, although later on we hear of striking exceptions to this line of conduct. Cicero thought this was one of the chief benefits of religion to the state. The breaking of a treaty with a foreign state was also an offence which it was expected that the gods would punish, as it involved the breaking of oaths and agreements.

Other offences which were direct affronts to a deity, such as the failure to perform a customary rite or sacrifice, or the theft of treasures or offerings from a shrine, were also believed to incur divine displeasure and punishment. For obscure reasons, incest and parricide (kin-murder) were also regarded as religious offences – perhaps because they aroused such deep repugnance, and being crimes committed within the family, they were particularly difficult to investigate. In general, therefore, although we can point to a number of offences which the Romans believed would be punished by the gods, the gods were not for the most part conceived of as the originators of the moral code, and of standards of conduct. This is perhaps one of the profoundest differences between the Christian and ancient Roman conception of religion.

RITES OF SACRIFICE AND DIVINATION

In the Republican period Roman religious observances can be divided into two main spheres of activity – the offering of sacrifices to the many gods, and the practice of divination. For it was believed that the goodwill and assistance of the gods could be procured and maintained by sacrifices and prayers, and that the will of the gods could to some extent be ascertained through divination and the interpretation of portents.

Romulus, the legendary founder and first king of Rome, was held to have instituted the practice of divination based on the flight of birds. Indeed, according to tradition, his choice of the site on which the city of Rome was to be built was shown to have the blessing of the gods by the flight of twelve vultures which he interpreted as a favourable omen. Numa, the second king of Rome, was credited with having established the custom of offering sacrifices to the gods. In fact, for the Romans of the later Republican period, the origins and significance of many of the religious rites and festivals, which were currently celebrated, were partially, or indeed wholly, mysterious. For the roots of many of their religious practices go back to the Bronze and Iron Ages, when the community consisted chiefly of farmers and shepherds; hence many of their religious rites were connected with agricultural processes and lost their meaning as the Romans became increasingly urbanized. However, the highly conservative Romans were reluctant to abandon any of the religious customs of their ancestors, even when the original significance had become obscure. The older religious rituals and customs were, the more they were venerated. Several of the characters in Cicero's dialogue *On the Nature of the Gods*, put forward this view. Says one:

> Belief in the gods of Rome has increased with time, and gathered strength and stability with the passing of the ages. We see that other beliefs being false and groundless have already fallen into oblivion with the lapse of time. Who now believes in Centaurs and Chimeras? For time destroys the fictions of error, while it confirms the determinations of nature and truth.

Later on, when a number of converts to Christianity spurned the traditional religion of Rome, one of the objections raised by the Romans to treating Christianity with toleration was that, unlike Judaism, it was not of sufficient antiquity to command respect; Suetonius, in his *Life of the Emperor Nero*, refers to Christians as adherents of 'a new and evil superstitition'.

We may now consider in greater detail these two important aspects of Roman religious practice – sacrifice and divination. To those brought up

The Sacred Way, looking towards the Arch of Titus in the Roman Forum. The Sacred Way was used as a processional route on religious occasions.

in the Christian tradition the idea of animal sacrifice is often highly repugnant; it is hard to recreate in the imagination with much sympathy the sounds and smells of such a sacrifice. This was often a messy business, sometimes arousing repulsion even in the ancient world. Lucian, a Greek from the east of the Empire writing in the second century AD, refers to 'the priest himself who stands there all bloody and like an ogre carves and pulls out entrails and extracts the heart and pours the blood about the altar'.

In fact not all the sacrifices performed by the Romans were of animals; many of the offerings made to the household gods by families at home were of cakes or wine, or milk. Literally, making a sacrifice meant making something holy, or sacred to the gods, that is, devoting it exclusively to their use. At the appropriate time of year, which was marked out by the Calendar, the chief gods of the state cults at Rome were all honoured by the sacrifice of domestic animals, as this was believed to be the most effective form of sacrifice. A phrase often used in the prayers accompanying such sacrifices, '*macte esto* – be thou greater or increased – suggests that the idea behind the offering of sacrifices was to transfer the life in the offering to the god. The most vital parts of the victim, the heart, liver, kidneys etc, were burned on the altar for the god, while the rest were eaten by the priests and worshippers. Probably in very early times the gods were thought of as actually consuming the parts of the animal offered to them; certainly in later times the offering of sacrifices was still believed to attract the attention of the god. For the philosopher Plutarch writes 'It is not the abundance of wine or the roasting of meat which makes the joy of festivals, but the good hope that the god is present in his benevolence, and graciously accepts what is offered.' Another prominent element in the offering of sacrificial animals to a god was undoubtedly the hope that the god would be induced to reciprocate the favour, and grant whatever the worshipper sought. Some sacrifices, however, were offered as an expiation for an offence or error, very often one in the carrying out of religious rites.

There were complex rules governing the choice of animal for the various gods; male animals were usually sacrificed to gods, and female ones to goddesses. Colour was sometimes considered important – black animals were thought appropriate in sacrifices to the gods of the underworld. Quite a variety of animals was used in sacrifice: oxen were often sacrificed to Jupiter, horses to Mars, and a red dog to Robigus, the deity who was believed to avert blight from the crops. At times of widespread anxiety and tension, and on state occasions of great importance, animal sacrifices on a huge scale might be vowed and carried out. After the disastrous defeat of the Roman army at Lake Trasimene by Hannibal in 217 BC three hundred oxen were vowed as a sacrifice to Jupiter. During the Principate the accessions and birthdays of the emperors might be marked by sacrifices on an enormous scale. Over 160,000 victims are said to have been sacrificed in the celebrations of public rejoicing which took place during the three months following the accession to the throne of the emperor Caligula in AD 37.

Elaborate rituals surrounded the act of sacrificing victims to the gods. Sacrifices might be offered on behalf of the state by the magistrates, or other state officials, as part of the official cult of a particular deity, or in thanksgiving for, or requesting, some particular favour for the Roman people. Similarly, private individuals might offer sacrifices to a deity either accompanying a request to a god, or as a thank-offering for a prayer fulfilled. The sacrifice was preceded by a procession of the worshippers and the victims, often accompanied by musicians, to the temple of the deity to be honoured; those taking part might wear special clothes and wreaths of laurel, and the animals might also be decorated with garlands and ribbons.

Sacrifice of the animals was usually carried out in the court in front of the temple at an altar specially provided for this purpose; the interior of a temple was obviously not a suitable place for the performance of blood sacrifices. In fact sometimes large decorated altars for sacrifice, such as the Altar of Augustan Peace, commemorating the peace brought to the Roman

Detail of a fresco from a tomb in the Isola Sacra cemetery near Ostia (see page 22), showing a youth making an offering.

world by Augustus and his safe return from Spain and Gaul, and the Altar of Augustan Piety vowed by the Senate in AD 22, when Livia, the widow of Augustus and the mother of Tiberius, was ill, were set up in isolation from any temple. The impressive colonnaded courts of the great temples of Rome, which provided the setting for important official sacrifices, can best be seen in the temple complexes of imperial date beyond the Roman Forum. Further afield, the magnificent Sanctuary of Jupiter Heliopolitanus at Baalbek, with its vast colonnaded forecourt containing the remains of a huge altar set in front of the façade of the temple, preserves something of the fine setting in which a sacrifice in Roman times took place.

The order of events leading up to the sacrifice of the animal victim seems to have gone like this. When the sacrificial procession reached the altar in front of the temple, those whose presence would profane the sacrifice were urged to depart (women and slaves were often excluded) and silence was enjoined on those who remained. Then the priests and those offering the sacrifice washed their hands, as ritual purity was required for making the worshipper acceptable to the god. The proceedings were accompanied by a flute player, whose music prevented any sounds from the outside which would invalidate the ritual from penetrating the sacred hush. Next, the priest or magistrate officiating covered his head with a fold of his toga, and took up a platter with a mixture of sacred flour and salt which he sprinkled on the head of the victim and on the sacrificial knife. Sometimes wine was also poured over the head of the animal from a shallow saucer-like vessel called a *patera*. An attendant then removed the ribbons and other decorations from the animal and drew a knife symbolically along its back, while whatever prayers or invocations were appropriate were offered by the individual suppliant or the officiating magistrate, who turned in the direction of the cult-statue within the temple. Then the attendant struck a blow with a hammer or an axe at the animal's head so that it fell to the ground and another attendant (*cultrarius* or slaughterer) cut the animal's throat. It was believed to be very inauspicious if the animal was not instantly killed, or if it attempted to run away, or if, after it was dismembered, its inner organs were found to be defective or malformed in any way. The inner organs were burnt on the altar to the god, but the other parts of the animal were eaten by the participants in a sacrificial meal. Small kitchens and dining-rooms were often built adjacent to temple precincts for the preparation and consumption of feasts following a sacrifice. When a large number of animals had been sacrificed a correspondingly large number of people would have shared in the subsequent feast. All the members of the Senate had the right to attend sacrificial banquets held on the Capitol at Rome, and it appears that in the provinces soldiers in the armies attended the sacrificial feasts, and sometimes got drunk during the festivities. For the poor, particularly those in the big cities, a sacrifice with many victims would have provided a rarely enjoyed chance to eat meat.

On many special religious occasions sacrifices were followed by the holding of public games, such as horse and chariot races, men's running races, and boxing and wrestling matches. The games were usually preceded by processions, in which images of the gods were carried before being set out on couches to watch the proceedings. Something of this tradition seems to have survived even down to recent times in parts of Italy and Spain, where images of the patron saint or of the Virgin Mary are carried through towns and villages on the appropriate feast day.

Although the important rite of sacrifice took place in front of, not inside, the temple, and although in Roman times the main altar was placed in front of the temple, not inside it, as is the altar in a Christian church, the temple buildings were not just empty shells forming a grandiose and symbolic backdrop to the rite of sacrifice, for they contained the cult statue of the deity of the temple. In antiquity, temples were taken to be the dwelling-places of the deities to whom they were dedicated, and the place of honour inside the temple was taken by the cult statue or statues of the deity or deities of the temple. The historian Tacitus tells of Pompey's astonish-

A marble altar with carved decoration, Ostia.

ment when, after the capture of Jerusalem in 63 BC, he seized the opportunity to enter the Temple of the Jews, and found that the Holy of Holies was empty, and without any image of the deity – 'an empty secret' he apparently called it (Tacitus, *Histories*, V, 9, 1).

The cult statues placed inside the temples were often larger than life-size, and fragments of a number of them have been recovered from the excavation of various temples. Roman generals, by their conquest of the Greek cities of southern Italy and Sicily, and later on the Greek mainland, acquired a vast quantity of Greek statuary for Rome, much of which was religious in character. The great influx of Greek works of art began, according to the historians of Rome, when Marcellus captured the rich Greek city of Syracuse in 211 BC. Later on, at the Triumph of Marcus Fulvius after his victory over the Aetolians in mainland Greece in 189 BC, 285 bronze statues and 230 marble statues were shown in the procession. Some of these were undoubtedly of gods; in fact there was a famous statue of Hercules for which Marcus Fulvius built a special temple, including in it nine Hellenistic statues of the Muses, and dedicating it to Hercules of the Muses. It became fashionable to include in the temples of Rome, in addition to the old cult images, statues imported from the sanctuaries of Greece which were thought to be the works of famous Greek sculptors.

The Temple of *Apollo in Circo,* which had originally been built in the fifth century BC, was eventually adorned with many Greek works of art: among these was a statue of Apollo in cedar wood taken from Seleucia in Syria, and twelve statues by a Rhodian sculptor, Philiscus, consisting of Apollo, Leto, Diana and the Nine Muses.

Although there is no explicit evidence, it may be that some people, particularly among the uneducated classes, thought that the statues of the gods in the temples were actually inhabited or possessed by the gods. Certainly the gods were believed to be so closely associated with their place of worship that their cults could not be transferred elsewhere. When the Romans contemplated moving from Rome after the sack of the city by the Gauls in 386 BC, they were dissuaded from making a move, so the story goes, by the argument that the feat of Jupiter could not be celebrated anywhere else except on the Capitol, that the good fortune of that site could not be transferred to any other place. The images of the gods of captured cities were often treated very much as if they were the gods themselves. Sometimes when the Romans captured a city they carried off the images of the gods of that city, partly so that those gods could no longer threaten the power of Rome. After the capture of Tarentum in 209 BC, the traditionalist Fabius Maximus did not try to move the colossal statues of the gods from the city, remarking that it was better to leave their angry gods to the inhabitants of Tarentum. In a similar spirit, Aemilius Paullus, when he visited the sanctuary of Olympia after his victory over Macedon and saw the enormous statue of Zeus by Phidias, is said to have felt himself in the actual presence of the god. In the early Christian period there is evidence that ordinary people thought the statues of the pagan gods really were the dwelling-places of evil spirits, and that the statues themselves had supernatural powers. These powers, apparently, were not so great as the power of the cross. There was a nude statue of the Greek goddess Aphrodite, an object of great veneration, in the centre of the town at Gaza; it seems that when, in AD 402, Bishop Porphyry, surrounded by Christians carrying crosses, approached this statue 'the demon who inhabited the statue, being unable to contemplate the terrible sign, departed from the marble with great tumult, and as he did so he threw the statue down and broke it into many pieces.'

The cult statues in the temples of Rome were often adorned with jewellery presented to them by grateful worshippers. In addition to gifts of precious ornaments, people also gave offerings of gold and silver to the deity of a temple. These were placed in a smaller room beyond the main room in which the cult statue stood. These gifts presented a great temptation to temple-robbers, notwithstanding the fact that the crime of robbing a temple was believed to be punishable by the gods themselves.

At certain times the temples were open to everyone, either for making petitions or for thanksgiving. Days of public prayer were decreed from time to time by the Senate, when the people, both men and women, wearing garlands and perhaps holding laurel branches, spent the whole day going round the temples of the city to salute the gods and give thanks for some fortunate turn of events. In exceptional circumstances several days of thanksgiving (*supplicationes*) might be decreed, as when Scipio Africanus defeated Hannibal at the battle of Zama in 202 BC. Apart from petitions or thanksgivings on behalf of the state, private individuals might also enter the *cella* of a temple in order to make a vow. It was customary for people to vow that if they were granted a certain prayer or request they would make an offering or sacrifice to the deity in return. The suppliant would write his request on a tablet and attach it to the cult statue. If the request was granted he might then set up an inscription (*ex-voto*) recording that he had happily discharged his vow.

In ancient Rome the observance of religious rituals and festivals took up a considerable amount of time and money. The official festivals were paid for by the state, although ambitious private individuals who wished to gain popular support might sometimes finance the games connected with the

Opposite : 'The Apotheosis of Homer'. This Hellenistic marble relief is signed by a sculptor of Priene, a Greek town in Asia Minor, but it was found near the Via Appia, south of Rome, so it was one of the large number of Greek works of art taken to Italy. It is an allegorical representation of the apotheosis of Homer, shown seated in the left corner. At the top, Zeus reclines on the summit of a mountain, and below him are the Nine Muses.

Above : Detail of the 'Apotheosis of Homer'. Allegorical figures approach a circular altar, on which one of them sprinkles incense. Behind the altar stands a bull, apparently the sacrificial victim. Animal sacrifices and offerings of incense were made to the gods by both the Greeks and the Romans.

festivals, or ostentatiously celebrate private sacrifices on a lavish scale. The Roman calendar, which we can reconstruct almost completely from various fragmentary inscriptions on which different parts of it are recorded, indicates that there were well over a hundred days in the year set aside for festivals (some occupied several days), so that the number of days on which law-suits could be heard and the assembly of the people could meet was limited. There were, however, no 'weekends', and not all festival days implied a complete suspension of public and private business.

There were far too many Roman festivals to discuss in detail, and in any case by the period of the late Republic a number of the more ancient and obscure festivals were celebrated only by the priests directly concerned with them. However, there were certain festivals, particularly those to which the celebration of public games was attached, which seem to have aroused great interest and enthusiasm. The new year was inaugurated with an impressive sacrifice to Jupiter Capitolinus, the patron god of the city. On 1 January the two new consuls, who were entering their year of office, having put on the special purple-bordered toga worn by the higher magistrates, set out from their houses in a procession, preceded by the lictors who carried the fasces, walking in single file. The two consuls and their supporters passed along the Sacred Way through the Forum, and climbed the Capitoline hill to the area in front of the Temple of Jupiter Optimus Maximus, where the consuls took their seats on their official ivory chairs, and received the acclaim of the crowds of spectators. Then the consuls sacrificed two white bulls to Jupiter in recognition of the vows made for the safety of the state on 1 January of the previous year, and renewed

Top and above: Roman theatre token, made of bone and found in Egypt. One side is decorated with the head of Hercules, while the letters on the reverse perhaps indicate the bearer's seat at the spectacle.

Right: Funerary relief of a magistrate responsible for organizing chariot races in the circus. The official and his wife are shown on the left of the relief. The husband is carved on a conspicuously larger scale than the other figures, no doubt to indicate his greater importance. Second century AD.

the vows for the coming year. The consuls then summoned the Senate to the first meeting of the year.

During February there were two important festivals, the Parentalia and the Lupercalia. The festival of the Parentalia lasted from 13 to 21 February, and was a time for honouring and commemorating the family dead, particularly parents. One of the Vestal Virgins inaugurated the ceremonies. During the period of the Parentalia all the temples of the city were closed and marriages could not be solemnized. Roman views about the after-life were rather hazy, and changed from time to time, but for the most part the Romans believed that the spirits of the dead, the Manes, remained more or less half-alive in or near their tombs, and that these ghosts required annual offerings of food and wine to placate them and prevent them from haunting the living; indeed meals were often buried with the dead in early times. During the Parentalia offerings of wine, milk and flowers were made by pious Romans at the tombs of their families on the outskirts of the great city; burials inside the city were not allowed. In *Fasti* (II, 535 ff.), Ovid touchingly describes the offerings that the Romans made to their dead:

> The ghosts ask but little: they value piety more than any expensive gift. . . . A tile wreathed with long garlands, a scattering of corn, a few grains of salt, bread soaked in wine, and a handful of violets: set these on a broken pot and leave it in the middle of the road.

During the Parentalia, on 15 February, the very ancient pastroal festival of the Lupercalia was held. Its origins are mysterious, although it appears to have been connected with promoting fertility. It is not even known for certain which god this festival honoured; Roman writers propose different candidates, but it was probably Faunus, a wild god of the countryside, as Ovid says. On this occasion, two teams of young men comprising the Luperci, or special priests of the festival, met in a cave called the Lupercal, on the Palatine hill, where according to tradition the she-wolf had suckled Romulus and Remus. Here the Luperci sacrificed three goats and a dog, and smeared their foreheads with the animals' blood. After a feast in the cave which was often a drunken and riotous celebration, the young men emerged dressed only in a strip of the skin of the slaughtered animals, and ran a race along the edge of the Palatine hill. As they went they whipped the spectators with thongs of the goat skins, a rite which may have been thought to promote fertility.

On 1 March, which in early times had marked the beginning of the Roman year, the sacred fire in the Temple of Vesta was rekindled by the Vestal Virgins, who carried out this ritual renewing of the fire by rubbing sticks together in the ancient manner. On this day also fresh laurel branches were fixed to the Regia, the residence of the *pontifex maximus* in Republican

Fragmentary relief of a Silenus offering a sacrifice at a blazing altar. He is wearing a garland, as human worshippers often did. Originating in Greek mythology, Sileni were the spirits of wild life in woodlands and hills. They were companions of Dionysus. With the growing influence of Greece on Rome, Sileni are also found in Roman art and literature. Ostia.

times, and to some of the other ancient religious buildings. March was the month sacred to Mars, the god of war, and during this time a number of ceremonies were carried out in his honour. The most important of these was the Dance of the Salii, priests of Mars, whose name means dancers or leapers. The Salii consisted of two groups of young patricians, who, dressed in embroidered tunics and short cloaks with red stripes, together with bronze breast-plates and conical helmets, armed with swords and spears, and carrying bronze shields shaped like a figure of eight, danced through the districts of Rome. The distinctive figure-of-eight shape of the shields is like that of the shields of the Mycenaeans of the Bronze Age, and strongly suggests that this ceremony goes back to very early times. Starting on the first of the month, and on other days later in the month, the Salii went in a procession through the city, doing a ritual dance and beating their shields with their swords. At certain places in the city they stopped to perform an elaborate dance and sing their ancient hymn, which was so old that the words were mostly unintelligible even to the performers, in the period of the late Republic. After their performances the Salii stayed in special lodgings, and enjoyed magnificent banquets. It is recorded that the greedy emperor Claudius, lured by the smell of roasting meats, once absented himself from public business in the Forum of Augustus to attend a banquet for the Salii going on in the nearby precincts of the Temple of Mars.

The Parilia, held on 21 April, was, in origin, like so many of Rome's festivals, agricultural. It was celebrated in honour of a deity or pair of deities, Pales – so obscure to Romans of late Republican times that not even the sex of the deity or deities was known, although there was a temple dedicated to Pales in Rome. The festival was originally concerned with purifying the flocks so as to keep them free from disease, but with the passing of time this festival was amalgamated with the celebrations for the birthday of Rome, which, according to tradition, fell on the same day. This festival was celebrated both publicly on an official level, and privately by shepherds in the countryside; there were also apparently private celebrations of the cult throughout the districts of the city of Rome, where the occasion was regarded as a time for drinking and making merry. Several Roman poets, including Ovid, describe how this festival was celebrated in the countryside; the sheepfold was sprinkled with water and swept out, and decorated with leaves, branches and a wreath. The sheep were then

fumigated with sulphur, and a fire of pine and olive branches was lit; offerings of cake and pails of milk were made, and the shepherd prayed for forgiveness if his sheep had strayed on to holy ground, or if he had entered or cut branches from a forbidden grove, or if he had disturbed any of the country deities. He prayed to Pales to keep disease and wolves away from his flocks, and for an increase in the number of his sheep, and in the milk and cheese they produced. Having made this prayer four times, washed in the dew, and drunk milk and wine, the shepherd leapt through the bonfire, perhaps with his flock following him. In the celebrations in the city a mixture of blood and ashes from the victims of previous sacrifices was preserved by the Vestal Virgins specially so that it could be burnt in the bonfires which were lit to celebrate this occasion in Rome. Here too the worshippers apparently leapt through the flames; Ovid claimed often to have taken part in these ceremonies.

During the last part of April games were held and a sacrifice was made in honour of Flora, originally the goddess of flowers, but later associated with fertility in general. These games lasted for several days, and began with a theatrical performance, which was apparently rather lewd. The games in the circus included the snaring of hares and goats, animals which were proverbial for their randiness. Vetches, beans and lupins were scattered among the crowds at the circus—again perhaps they were regarded as symbols of fertility. Not surprisingly, this festival seems to have attracted a more than usually ribald crowd of spectators, and gave rise to obscene jokes and entertainments, or so numerous Roman writers complain.

Some time during May, for it was a 'movable feast' not celebrated on the same date every year, there was an important festival for purifying the fields and keeping them free of harmful influences. At this festival the farmer would lead the victims for the sacrifice three times round the boundaries of his land before sacrificing them to Ceres, or sometimes to Mars. Cato, writing on agriculture, prescribes that the victims should be a pig, a bull and a sheep, known as *suovetaurilia*, but the poets Virgil and Tibullus suggest that in many cases only one victim was offered, perhaps a lamb. Virgil writes (*Georgics*, I, 343 ff.):

> All the farm labourers should pray to Ceres, and offer milk, honey and sweet wine. Then the victim should be led three times round the new crops, attended by the whole crowd singing and praying.

This procession round the boundaries of a farm seems to be akin to the medieval custom of 'beating the bounds' of the parish in May, when the priest and his parishioners would go in a procession round the boundaries of the parish praying for the preservation of the parish and the produce of its fields. No doubt many pious farmers kept up the celebration of this ritual into late Republican times and beyond. There was a similar public festival at which perhaps in early times the victims were led right round the territory of Rome to purify and protect it. However, as the city grew larger this was no longer possible, and in the time of Augustus at any rate sacrifices were held at a number of places outside the city which were regarded as boundaries. Known as the Ambarvalia, this festival was probably celebrated in its public form in Rome by the college of priests called the Arval Brethren.

The procession round the fields was called a *lustratio*, from *luere*, to loose or set free, because it was believed that the sacrifice of these victims would keep the crops free from harm. A similar sacrifice called a *lustrum*, and traditionally consisting of a pig, a sheep and a bull was carried out in Rome supposedly every five years after the taking of the census. In late Republican times the taking of the census was allowed to lapse, but it was revived by Augustus, who celebrated the *lustrum* three times.

Among the Romans human sacrifice seems to have been relatively rare, although it was practised by their neighbours; the sacrifice of children was a regular feature of the religious rites of the inhabitants of Carthage,

Tombs along the Via Appia, south of Rome. Under Roman law, burial had to be outside the city, so tombs were often erected along roads just outside the city.

the hated enemy of Rome. However, at a time of great public stress and anxiety after the disastrous battle of Cannae in 216 BC, when the Romans were defeated by the Carthaginians led by Hannibal, the Romans sacrificed two Greeks and two Gauls, burying them alive in the *Forum Boarium*. But in general human sacrifice was regarded with abhorrence by the Romans; Livy described it as 'a quite un-Roman rite'. The religious toleration generally practised by the Romans was not extended to the Druids of Gaul, in part because they were associated with the savage and horrific practice of human sacrifice. Human sacrifice was legally prohibited at Rome in 97 BC. However, some of the religious rites celebrated at Rome were such as to suggest that the rites as originally celebrated had involved the sacrifice of human beings. For example on 14 or 15 May, the date is not certain, there was a great procession including the Vestal Virgins and some priests and magistrates, which went around the city to twenty-seven small shrines known as the *Sacraria Argeorum*, collecting from them rush-puppets resembling old men, which had been deposited in these shrines two months earlier. These the Vestal Virgins proceeded to throw into the River Tiber from the oldest bridge, the Pons Sublicius. Some Romans and others who saw the ritual thought that these effigies were surrogates for the old men thrown into the river in early times as a sacrifice to the ancient god Saturn. There was a proverb current in Rome, 'Off the bridge with the sixty year olds', which may back up this interpretation.

During June, rituals connected with the important shrine of Vesta in the Roman Forum were celebrated; from 7 June, married women were for eight days allowed to enter the shrine to worship, and they apparently came barefoot to the temple carrying simple offerings of food. At the festival of Vesta on 9 June the Vestal Virgins made offerings to the goddess of the special cake, or *mola salsa*, which they prepared according to ancient formulae from grain and salt. At any rate this day came to be regarded as a holiday for bakers and millers. Ovid recounts that the asses that turned the mills were garlanded with flowers and decorated with loaves, and the mill stones strewn with clover. On 15 June the Vestal Virgins cleaned out their shrine, and carried all the rubbish from it to the river.

On 24 June there was a popular festival of Fors Fortuna, or Fortune, at a temple on the banks of the River Tiber downstream from Rome, to which people flocked on foot or by boat. Ovid exhorts people to enjoy this festival, and urges them not to be ashamed of drinking excessively in the flower-garlanded boats that carry them to the temple. Fortune was a popular goddess, particularly with the poorer classes, and her cult was one in which slaves were allowed to participate.

In August a sacrifice to Hercules was celebrated at one of his shrines in the city, perhaps the old round temple near the Circus Maximus. Hercules was the patron of many Roman businessmen, and it became customary for them to dedicate a tithe of their profits to him in gratitude for his protection. Sometimes this practice was emulated by the very wealthy, like Sulla and Crassus, who perhaps hoped to gain the support and admiration of the people by this means. Indeed Plutarch recounts that when Sulla dedicated a tenth of his fortune to Hercules it enabled such lavish feasts to be produced for days on end for the people of Rome that a great quantity of food had to be thrown into the river at the end of each day. He adds that the wine which was provided was at least forty years old.

Towards the end of August the festival of the very ancient god Consus (whose name indicates that he was originally god of the grain-store) was celebrated by a sacrifice at his subterranean altar at the lower end of the Circus Maximus, and by games held in the Circus. According to popular tradition it was while the Sabines were watching these games (in the time of the kings) that the Romans were able to carry off their women. At the time of this festival it became the custom to garland horses and mules in the city, and allow them a day of rest. Something of this tradition seems to have survived in Rome into relatively recent times; Goethe comments (*Italian Journey*, Pt I) that when he was in Rome in 1788, St Antony had become

Another tomb, dating from the Roman imperial period, along the Via Appia.

Tombs were often richly decorated with sculpture reflecting the means and taste of the deceased. This tomb of a freedwoman, Naevoleia Tyche, outside Pompeii, is decorated with acanthus scrolls and a relief of a ship entering harbour. The ship with furled sails is possibly a symbol of death, echoing Cicero's words, 'The nearer I come to the hour of death, the more I feel like a man who has sighted land, and who knows he will soon enter harbour after his long voyage'.

the patron saint of all four-footed creatures:

... and his feast is a saturnalia for these otherwise oppressed animals ... The gentry must either walk or stay at home ... Horses and mules, their manes and tails gorgeously braided with ribbons, are led up to a small chapel, and a priest armed with an enormous brush sprinkles them with holy water.

From the 5th to the 19th of September the *Ludi Romani* (Roman Games) in honour of Jupiter were held, and on the 13th, which was believed to be the anniversary of the founding of the temple, one of the consuls conducted a sacrifice in honour of Jupiter Optimus Maximus at his temple on the Capitol. The sacrifice was followed by an enormous banquet for the magistrates and senators at which images of Jupiter, Juno and Minerva were set out on couches as if to share in the feast.

During November the Plebeian Games were celebrated; these were preceded by a great procession from the Capitol through the Forum to the Circus Maximus. This procession consisted not only of the competitors, wrestlers, runners, boxers and charioteers, but also of clowns, musicians

and dancers, and of images of the gods which were carried shoulder-high on stretchers; on arrival at the Circus the images were set out on couches to watch the Games.

Some time during December, the date varied from year to year, the women of Rome, or at least the more important ones, led by the Vestal Virgins, celebrated the rites of Bona Dea, the Good Goddess, in the house of one of the principal magistrates – circumstances which sometimes gave rise to scandal. In 62 BC the ceremony was held in Julius Caesar's house, and Publius Clodius, a young patrician of dubious morals, gained access to the house from which all men had been formally excluded, disguised as a woman and carrying a lute; it was said that Clodius did this because he was carrying on a love affair with Caesar's wife, Popeia. Clodius's presence was betrayed by his deep voice, and the ceremonies were brought to an abrupt end, and had to be repeated later. Caesar divorced his wife, and Clodius was put on trial for sacrilege. Bona Dea was most probably an earth-goddess, who was believed to promote fertility in women. This cult had something in common with the mystery religions, in that details of the sacred rites could not be revealed, and the real name of the goddess was kept secret, while the celebration of the rites included the unveiling of sacred objects which could be shown only to the women participants. Bona Dea seems to have been a popular goddess; there was a temple dedicated to her on the Aventine hill, where in May the sacrifice of a sow was made to her.

On 17 December, the greatest holiday of the year, the feast of the Saturnalia, was celebrated. Although the religious rites took place only on the 17th, the holiday period was gradually extended – by Cicero's time it lasted for seven days. This was the time when all the familiar distinctions of Roman society were overturned; it was a time of freedom for household slaves who were waited on by their masters at table. People exchanged presents, and it was the one time in the year when people were allowed to play gambling games in public. In large households it was customary for the members to elect a mock king or master of the revels to organize the festivities, a custom which used to be continued at Twelfth Night. The precise function of the god Saturn, in whose honour this festival was held, was obscure, even in antiquity. He may have been a god of Etruscan origin, but in time he came to be identified with the Greek Cronus, the father of Zeus, and so his name became synonymous with 'the good old days', or a vanished Golden Age. The remains of his temple are still visible on the edge of the Forum at the foot of the Capitoline hill, and it was here that the celebration of the festival began with a sacrifice to the god, made in the Greek manner, with those presiding having uncovered heads. The sacrifice was attended by the members of the Senate, and it was followed by a great banquet. Some austere and priggish Romans avoided joining in the fun and celebrations of a festival such as this; the Younger Pliny built himself a secluded apartment in his villa at Laurentum where he slipped away from such festivities, while Seneca's advice was to devote the period of the Saturnalia to serious study rather than to idle pleasure. In general, however, this festival was a season of good-will and conviviality, and something of the atmosphere and traditions of the Saturnalia appear to have been taken over by the early Christians in the celebrations following Christ's Nativity.

Divination, as mentioned earlier, was the other fundamental element in the official religion of Rome. It was believed that by means of divination men could ascertain the will of the gods, and so find out whether a proposed course of action was favoured by them. Divination was not a method of directly predicting future events. Several means of divination were practised; the most ancient Roman method, going back to the time of the kings, was by observation of the flight and calls of birds, which was known as augury, and lay in the care of the augurs. Later, divination by means of the inspection of the entrails of the sacrificial victims, and by the observance of prodigies and portents, such as monstrous births and natural disasters,

Opposite and above : Statues of Vestal Virgins in the House of the Vestals in the Forum in Rome. In addition to being responsible for maintaining the cult of Vesta, goddess of the Hearth, the Vestals took part in religious festivals in honour of many of the other deities of Rome.

51

The coast of Agnano, looking towards Pozzuoli (Puteoli). This coastal stretch was a fashionable area for seaside villas in Roman times.

The wooded area of Cuma, a well-known oracle site.

was also practised. Faith in and enthusiasm for one particular method of divination rather than another seems to have varied at different times in Roman history. However, the efficacy of the practice as a whole does not appear to have been questioned except by a few tough-minded politicians, and by a few intellectuals such as Cicero, who wavered in his opinion, setting out the arguments both for and against the practice in his dialogue *On Divination*.

Although most Romans were extremely attentive to, or, as it might seem to us, credulous about, signs and omens, there were always some people who disregarded them. Claudius Marcellus, the consul in 222 BC and the veteran of many successful military campaigns, is reputed always to have been carried to battle in a closed litter so that he avoided seeing any unfavourable omens; he was not otherwise irreligious, as he dedicated temples in Rome to *Honos* and *Virtus*. It was, in fact, a curious Roman doctrine that unfavourable omens did not count for anything if they were not formally observed. However, those who disregarded the omens when

they had been observed, and then met with disaster, were felt by traditionalists to exemplify the truth of divination; for example, the triumvir Marcus Crassus left Rome in 54 BC for a campaign against the Parthians in spite of a warning that the omens were unfavourable; in the ensuing battle at Carrhae Crassus himself was killed and the Roman army suffered a tremendous defeat. And when, during the First Punic War, Publius Claudius Pulcher, disregarding the inauspicious omens produced by the sacred chickens refusing to eat, engaged in a battle in which the greater part of his fleet was destroyed, this disaster too was taken to illustrate the importance and efficacy of divination.

Divination by augury, that is, predicting the attitude of the gods from the flight and calls of birds, was a complicated and supposedly secret process known only to those who were elected augurs, so the procedures cannot now be reconstructed in detail. It appears, however, that crows, ravens and owls were believed to give signs by their calls and singing, and eagles and vultures by their flight. Cicero recounts that in ancient times augury was so highly regarded that there was no matter of importance, even relating to private business, which was transacted without taking the auspices. In Rome, taking the auspices was accomplished by the appropriate magistrate going with one of the members of the College of Augurs to a special site on the Capitol known as the *auguraculum*, where the augur, having first directed the magistrate to watch a certain quarter of the sky, would interpret any signs reported by the magistrate. In military campaigns, where there might be a shortage of birds at a critical moment, chickens were carried in cages with the armies so that the required auspices could be taken hurriedly before engaging in a battle or crossing a river. Pieces of cake were thrown to the chickens, and if as they fed any crumbs fell from their beaks to the ground it was considered a favourable omen. This practice seems to have been something of an innovation in the ancient religious traditions, and not surprisingly it occasionally aroused scepticism; one of the speakers in Cicero's dialogue *On Divination* (II, 35) comments:

> When a miserable bird is kept in a cage and is ready to die of hunger –
> if such a one when pecking up its food happens to let some particle fall,
> can you think that this is an auspice? Do you believe that Romulus
> consulted the god in this manner?

It seems that with the passing of time the Romans gradually became less conscientious about taking the auspices on all the appropriate occasions, for there are plenty of references to contemporary neglect of this rite in Cicero's dialogue. The taking of the auspices and other functions of the augurs came to be more or less confined to dealing with the religious aspects of holding assemblies. Before the day on which an assembly of the people was to be held the magistrate who was to preside would pitch a tent at the place where the assembly was to take place, and watch the sky for signs. Other magistrates too were entitled to report signs if they happened to observe them; in addition to signs from birds, lightning was an unfavourable omen which could be reported. If the presiding magistrate or an augur saw an unfavourable sign the meeting could not take place, or it was called off if it had already started. If the sign was seen by a private individual the presiding magistrate decided whether to accept it. During the last years of the Republic the taking of the auspices and the observation of signs seems sometimes to have been used, or rather misused, by means of finding unfavourable omens, to prevent the carrying of legislation in the popular assembly, or the holding of elections.

In the later years of the Republic divination by means of the observation of birds appears to have given way in popularity to the forms of divination practised by the *haruspices*, or soothsayers. The most important function of the *haruspices* was to inspect and interpret the entrails of sacrificial victims so as to determine whether the sacrifice was acceptable to the god, and whether a proposed course of action was favoured by the god. Since this

Above and right : The rock-hewn tunnel leading to the cave of the Cumaean Sibyl, near Pozzuoli. There were a number of Sibyls in the Greco-Roman world, whose prophecies were delivered in an ecstatic trance and written down on palm leaves. The visit of Aeneas to the cave of the Cumaean Sibyl and his descent with her into the underworld were vividly described by Virgil.

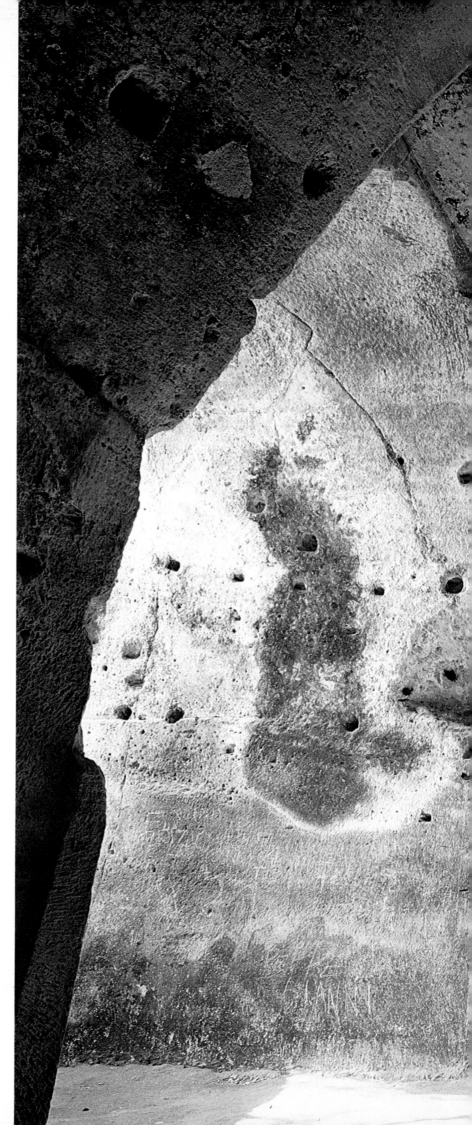

View from Cuma to the sea.

form of divination was Etruscan in origin, at first all those who practised it in Rome were Etruscans. For a long period they were somewhat despised as foreign barbarians, and were viewed with scepticism; in the second century BC Cato is said to have expressed surprise that one *haruspex* could pass another in the street without winking at him. However, during that century the practice of consulting *haruspices* became more common, until eventually they apparently assumed a greater importance than the augurs.

The *haruspices* most commonly carried out divination in the following way: after an animal had been killed as a sacrifice to a god it was handed over to the *haruspex* who examined it to see if its internal organs were perfect and unblemished. Deformities in certain parts of the animal's internal organs seem to have been taken as an indication that a particular god was angry.

Haruspices were often in demand to undertake divination for private citizens, and they seem to have charged considerable fees for their services. By the time of the early Empire they were so popular that the emperor Tiberius took steps to regulate their activities, and decreed that they could only engage in divination before witnesses, so as to minimize the chances of deliberate deception. *Haruspices* were professional experts in their craft of divination, unlike the other groups of people at Rome who practised divination, the augurs and the Board of Fifteen Keepers of the Sibylline Books, who were simply prominent citizens. Apart from deliberately seeking signs from the gods by examining the entrails of sacrificial victims, the *haruspices* might also be called on to interpret unexplained or unusual natural phenomena such as floods of the Tiber, earthquakes, comets or an

58

eclipse, or apparently supernatural phenomena such as shields sweating blood, the statue of a god weeping or a cow talking. These sights would be reported to the Senate who would then consult the *haruspices* as to which gods were angry, and how they could be appeased by religious rites; this was known as the expiation of portents. In times of public stress and military reverses, reports of portents and prodigies tended to be more numerous than at other times. Their occurrence was meticulously recorded by the traditionalist historian Livy, and even the more critical Tacitus gives some account of them, while Suetonius, the popular historical biographer of the Caesars, accords them great prominence. Such constant reporting of these phenomena indicates that many Romans did take them seriously.

In addition to the augurs and the *haruspices*, the Romans also consulted the Sibylline Books to discover the will of the gods, although more rarely; consultation of the Sibylline Books was reserved for special occasions. These books were reputed to have come from the old Greek colony of Cuma just north of Naples, the legendary dwelling of the famous Cumaean Sibyl, to whom the books were attributed. At Rome the books were kept at first in the Temple of Jupiter on the Capitol, under the care of a Board of Ten, which was later increased to fifteen, through whom consultation of the Books took place on command from the Senate. The original Sibylline Books allegedly consisted of the prophecies of the Cumaean Sibyl written on palm leaves in Greek hexameter verses. After these had been destroyed in the fire which burnt down the Temple of Jupiter in 83 BC, a new collection of the prophecies of the Sibyl was compiled from the records of her utterances kept in various sanctuaries in Greece. The statements in these Books carried great weight, and they were consulted over a long period of time. The first collection of the Sibylline Books was reputedly acquired from the Sibyl herself by Tarquinius Priscus, the fifth king of Rome in the late seventh century BC, and the Books were still consulted in the fourth century AD – a span of almost a thousand years.

The Sibylline Books were consulted at times of crisis, and seem to have been responsible for the introduction of a number of Greek religious customs to Rome, and for the introduction of new cults. At the time of a great plague in 399 BC during the war against Veii they prescribed the holding of the first *lectisternium*, a ritual consisting of providing for the participation of the gods at sacrificial feasts by setting out their images on couches at the meal. Later, in the Punic Wars, the books counselled the introduction to Rome of the cult of the Great Mother (Magna Mater) from Phrygia in order to secure victory against Hannibal, and so the mysterious black stone which was the emblem or fetish of the Great Mother was brought from Pessinus in Phrygia to Rome.

Although all these forms of divination and sacrifice may seem bizarre to us, and the scepticism with which they were sometimes viewed well founded, they undoubtedly performed several useful functions for the Roman state. By means of divination to ensure the favour and co-operation of the gods in the affairs of the state, the confidence of the public in the officials of the Roman state could be maintained in difficult circumstances, or more easily restored after military defeats. The fact that the elected magistrates and officials, particularly commanders on the battlefield, took the auspices or consulted the *haruspices* after sacrificing must have added to their authority, and increased public confidence in whatever decision was made, as it could be seen to be favoured by the gods. In times of trouble, a commander's willingness to propitiate the gods in response to alarming portents, and to make sacrifices on an impressive scale, might assist in restoring public confidence and help to avert panic and loss of morale. Moreover, the pomp and ceremonial surrounding the rituals of divination and sacrifice would have increased peoples' awe and respect for the magistrates and generals. Hence, although the religious rituals of sacrifice and divination did not work for the Romans in the way that they believed, these rituals nevertheless did function for the good of the Roman state and its people by fostering political cohesion and stability.

An empty throne, called the 'Lansdowne Throne', as it formed part of the Lansdowne collection of antiquities. This large marble throne, which dates from the late first century BC, or the first century AD, was partially restored in the eighteenth century. Covered by a cloak, and with a snake, box and quiver carved on it, the throne symbolizes the power of a deity, perhaps Apollo; a carved relief depicting the Temple of Cybele in Rome shows a similar empty throne set under the apex of the pediment.

AUGUSTUS'S RELIGIOUS REVIVAL

We must now consider the life and achievements of the emperor Augustus, since he instituted important and far-reaching religious reforms, which took effect throughout the Roman world. The rise of Octavian, later called Augustus, to supreme power in the Roman world marked the end of a century of disorder, often degenerating into anarchy, in the management of Rome's government and affairs of state. The culmination of the period of the breakdown of law and order had been the fourteen years of civil war which followed the murder of Julius Caesar in 44 BC by Brutus and Cassius and their adherents, who aimed to restore the ancient, but now decayed and obsolete, Republican institutions of Rome. The murder of Caesar had been sparked off by persistent rumours and intimations that he was aiming to become king and finally to subvert the tottering Republican constitution. Octavian, Caesar's great nephew, who was named as chief heir in Caesar's will, vowed to avenge the murder, and combined with Mark Antony (Marcus Antonius) and Lepidus to form a triumvirate, or committee of three, 'to restore the state'. In the ensuing proscriptions 2000 Romans were killed, including Cicero, and many of the victims seem to have been purged because their opponents coveted their possessions or property, rather than for political reasons. The triumvirs defeated the forces of Brutus and Cassius at the battle of Philippi in 42 BC, and Brutus and Cassius committed suicide.

Lepidus, the third member of the triumvirate, was soon forced to retire into private life, and Antony and Octavian remained in uneasy partnership, each considering himself the rightful heir to the Caesarian cause. Octavian consolidated his hold over the west of the Empire, settling veterans in Italy, and undertaking military campaigns in Illyricum and Dalmatia, while in the east Antony attempted to deal with the threat of a Parthian invasion in Asia Minor, and was less successful. Soon Antony's alleged marriage to Cleopatra, the queen of Egypt, and his gifts of additional territories to her, provided Octavian with a pretext for declaring war. Octavian decisively defeated the fleet of Antony and Cleopatra in a battle at Actium off the coast of Epirus in 31 BC; Antony and Cleopatra fled to Egypt where they too committed suicide.

Octavian was left undisputed master of the Roman world; the rule of one man was now accepted as inevitable, and most survivors of the old governing class considered the end of the civil war and the restoration of peace ample compensation for their loss of political power. The war-weariness of the Romans at this time is powerfully expressed in literature. While the fighting was still going on, Horace wrote a poem suggesting that the Romans should abandon their city for some remote and far-off place where they could get away from the horrors of war. Some lines of Virgil (*Georgics*, I, 511–14, trans. C. Day Lewis) express the feeling that wars and fighting had somehow got quite out of control:

The interior of the Pantheon, Rome, which was originally built in the reign of Augustus, but rebuilt under Hadrian. Dedicated to all the gods, this temple has a soaring dome which rises to a height of 142 feet above the floor, and seems to echo the dome of the heavens.

Left : Fragmentary fresco showing the god Apollo. He is seen here with a lyre, as was appropriate to the god of music and poetry. Augustus paid particular honour to Apollo, and promoted his cult as a god of peace.

The wicked war-god runs amok through all the world:
So when racing chariots have rushed from the starting gate,
They gather speed on the course and the driver tugs at the curb-rein
His horses run away, car out of control, quite helpless.

Romans who had lived through the atrocities of the civil wars tried to find some explanation of why they had suffered such calamities, and they seem to have taken refuge in the traditional explanation for public disasters – that they were sent by the gods as a punishment for the neglect of religion, or failure in the performance of rituals and religious ceremonies. During the period of fighting and anarchy, temples had been allowed to fall into ruin, priesthoods had gone unfilled, and some ceremonies and rites had been allowed to lapse, or had been cynically manipulated for political reasons. Horace puts forward this explanation: 'You will continue to pay for the sins of your fathers, O Roman, until you restore the ruined temples of the gods, and their images filthy with black smoke' (*Odes*, III, 6, 1). This view seems to be implicit also in much of Livy's historical writing; he complains of the neglect of the gods in his own period, and insists that it was the observance of even inessential religious rites and customs that had made Rome great in the past.

Augustus appears to have shared and to have exploited the conviction that a revival of traditional religious customs and observances was necessary for the recovery of peace and harmony in the Roman world. There was a widespread expectation current through much of the earlier part of the century, that a new era which would be a second Golden Age was about to begin. This belief was expressed in the famous Fourth Eclogue of Virgil, which foretold the birth of a boy under whose rule the world would enjoy peace and a miraculous Golden Age. (Later on, after Christianity became the religion of Rome in the fourth century AD, it was believed that in this poem Virgil had predicted the birth of Christ, and so Virgil was given something of the same status as the prophets of the Old Testament, who had also foretold the birth of Christ.) Augustus, however, saw the hope of the new Golden Age as having immediate relevance; he grasped the opportunity afforded by this hope of a new era among people after the civil wars, and vigorously promoted a religious revival.

The most urgent task was the repair and restoration of many crumbling religious buildings. Not long after the battle of Actium, in his sixth consulate (28 BC), Augustus, as he proudly recounts in his memoirs, the *Res Gestae*, restored eighty-two temples in the city of Rome. This shows how serious the problem of the neglect of religious buildings had become.

Right : Head of Augustus from a colossal bronze statue, probably made in Egypt. The whites of the eyes are inlaid with marble, the irises with glass. The image of the emperor was diffused throughout the provinces in sculpture and on coins. This head was found beyond the frontiers of the Empire at Meroe in the Sudan ; it had probably been taken as booty by Ethiopian tribesmen after a raid on Roman Egypt.

Above: *Marble bust of the emperor Hadrian, who ruled from AD 117 to 138. Hadrian travelled widely throughout the empire, reorganizing administration and defence. Under Hadrian a number of important buildings were constructed, including the Pantheon and his famous villa near Tibur (Tivoli). This bust was found in the villa.*

Archaeological evidence, too, indicates that a considerable number of temples in Rome were restored, or even rebuilt during the reign of Augustus, among them the Temple of Saturn and the Temple of Divus Julius in the Forum, the Temple of *Apollo in Circo*, and the Temple of Magna Mater on the Palatine. Augustus also built two new temples, the Temple of Apollo on the Palatine, and the great Temple of Mars Ultor set in the Forum of Augustus. This large-scale restoration and building of temples made extensive use of marble, and Suetonius quotes Augustus as boasting that he had found Rome built of sun-dried bricks, and left her clothed in marble.

As we have seen, the traditional religion of Rome was very much the official religion of the state, and was closely connected with the city's institutions and forms of government. When Augustus became virtually sole ruler of the Roman world a profound transformation of the state and society took place. Although Augustus was careful to keep up a façade of government by the Senate, there was in fact a fundamental change in the nature of the Roman state – the change from Republic to Monarchy. Augustus took care never to claim the title of 'king', which was hateful to the Romans; he preferred to be known simply as *princeps*, leading states-man, and to seem to be merely *primus inter pares*, first among equals. The Senate continued to meet, but only to sponsor the measures he had proposed to it, and the Assembly of the People met to pass such measures, while the Voting Assemblies met to appoint his candidates. Augustus was effectively in control because he was in command of the frontier provinces of the Empire where most of the legions were stationed. The settlement which Augustus imposed on the governing classes of Rome, with its pretence of continuing the Republican form of government, although resented by some, appears to have been largely taken at face value; the historian, Velleius Paterculus, writing in the early first century AD, com-mented on the settlement: 'The Roman world was at peace, the laws were again enforced. . . . The traditional state of the Republic was restored.' As might be expected, given the close interdependence between state and religion in the Roman world, the political transformation of the state was reflected by changes and modifications in religion. As was the case with political changes, religious changes were often masked by their apparent or superficial conformity with traditional religious practices and institu-tions.

The Roman emperors after Augustus came to assume a central place in the cults of the official religion of Rome and of the Empire; the deification of many of the emperors and the gradual establishment of emperor worship throughout the Empire was to add a new and important dimension to the state religion. These profound changes in religion attendant upon the setting up of a monarchical form of government did not all come about under Augustus; his position was transitional between the disintegration of Republican government and the full establishment of imperial rule. Nevertheless, in Augustus's time we can discern tendencies in religious observances and institutions which point in the direction of future developments in religion, and which indicate something of a shift in the religious mentality of the Roman people.

One of the ways in which Augustus was able to influence and even to manipulate, for his own ends, religious feeling in Rome was by the choice of the deities to whom he paid special devotion. By singling out certain deities to honour, Augustus was able to buttress his own position, emphas-izing his special relationship with the gods, and his important historical role. The two gods to whom he showed particular devotion were Apollo and Mars.

It appears that Augustus genuinely believed that he enjoyed the special protection of the god Apollo. In claiming the personal protection of one particular god he was following a well-established precedent among prominent Romans; Scipio Africanus was credited with a special relation-ship with Jupiter, while Julius Caesar had claimed a special relationship with Venus Genetrix, and Sulla with both Venus and Apollo. According to Suetonius, after Augustus's house had been struck by lightning, he vowed to build a temple to Apollo on the Palatine hill in Rome, adjacent to the house. Augustus's great victory at the battle of Actium was won in the vicinity of a Temple to Apollo, which he proceeded to restore; Apollo, he claimed, had appeared to him at a decisive moment in the battle. After the victory, Augustus built the Temple to Apollo on the Palatine in Rome, and added to it two fine libraries of Greek and Latin books, and a portico in which Greek sculpture was displayed. He transferred to the new temple the Sibylline Books from the Temple of Jupiter on the Capitol, and deposited them under the cult statue of Apollo in two gilt coffers.

Apollo had not been a particularly prominent god in Rome before Augustus's time, although he was a major god among the Greeks, with great sanctuaries at Delos and Delphi. His cult had been imported to Rome in the fifth century BC during a plague, because he was regarded as a god of healing. Augustus's particular devotion to him was no doubt founded partly on personal conviction, and partly on various associations which had come to be made with Apollo and which it suited Augustus to promote. In poetry, Apollo is several times given an important role in the creation of a new era and the inauguration of a second Golden Age, and Augustus wanted to associate himself with this process, and to appear as the founder of the new order. Rumours even circulated that Augustus was actually a son of Apollo, Apollo in the form of a snake having had intercourse with Augustus's mother exactly ten months before his birth, when she inadvertently fell asleep in his temple during an evening ceremony. It also appears that by this time Apollo had come to be regarded as a god of peace, and of civilization, and these were undoubtedly ideals which Augustus wanted to promote and foster. The great Centennial Festival, or *Ludi saeculares*, which Augustus celebrated in 17 BC, was traditionally held about every hundred years to mark the end of an epoch. Augustus, by offering the sacrifices for this festival during three successive days and nights, hoped to associate himself in popular opinion with the ending of the old era and the initiating of a great new age. The festival ended with celebrations at the new Temple of Apollo where a choir of twenty-seven boys and twenty-seven girls sang a hymn, the *Carmen Saeculare*, specially commissioned by Augustus from Horace for the occasion, honouring Apollo and celebrating the return of peace and the restoration of ancient morality.

Augustus also paid exceptional honours to Mars, the god of war, and again he had particular personal reasons for doing so; in 42 BC, in the campaign leading up to the battle of Philippi, Augustus had vowed a temple to Mars the Avenger, if he should succeed in avenging the murder of his adoptive father, Julius Caesar. Mars, the god of war, had for a long time been highly honoured by the Romans; a month had been named after him, and his altar stood in the Campus Martius, a low-lying plain between the Capitol and Palatine hills and the River Tiber. Here military exercises, and horse-racing in honour of the god took place. However, until the time of Augustus there was no temple of Mars built within the city of Rome; he was perhaps regarded as a wild and savage spirit, whom it was best to keep at some distance. Augustus chose to honour him, as Mars the Avenger, by building a magnificent temple to him within the ancient city boundaries, on a site between the Forum of Julius Caesar and the crowded tenement quarter of the Subura.

The adornment of the forum in front of the temple was designed to be more than an inspiring reminder of Rome's greatness; statues of famous ancestors of Julius Caesar and Augustus were included in its decoration, while a statue of Julius Caesar was set inside the temple together with the statues of Mars, the titular deity, and Venus, the ancestress of the Julian house. Thus the whole building complex became something of a dynastic showpiece and exercise in propaganda, emphasizing Augustus's connections by blood or in spirit with the great men of Rome's past, and by these

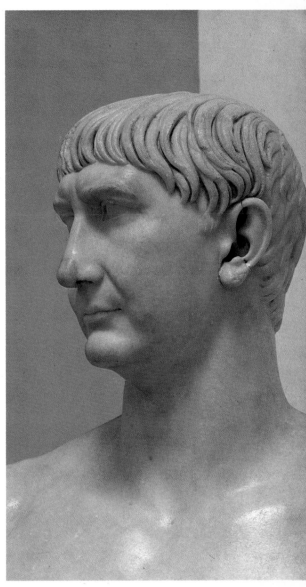

Marble bust of the emperor Trajan, who ruled from AD 97 to 117. His remains were buried beneath the famous column in Rome on which his victories in the Dacian campaign were depicted. Under Trajan, Rome was at the height of her power, and the Empire reached its widest extent.

means claiming continuity between the era of the Republic and his newly instituted rule as *princeps*. Very much the same message is evoked by Virgil in the Sixth Book of the *Aeneid* (trans. Dryden), where his well-known catalogue of the ancient kings of Rome and of the heroes of the Republic gives great prominence to Augustus:

> But next behold the youth of form divine,
> Caesar himself exalted in his line;
> Augustus promis'd oft, and long foretold,
> Sent to the realm that Saturn ruled of old;
> Born to restore a better age of gold.
> Afric and India shall his power obey,
> He shall extend his propagated sway,
> Beyond the solar year, without the starry way.

A similar message is enshrined in the *Ara Pacis Augustae*, or Altar of Augustan Peace, which was erected in the Campus Martius between 13 and 9 BC, to celebrate Augustus's safe return to Rome after a long absence in Gaul and Spain. In this monument Augustus was able to link the traditions and myths of Rome's past with himself, and to portray the peace and plenty which his rule had brought to Italy.

In addition to restoring and building temples and other religious edifices, Augustus also took measures to fill all the vacant places in the colleges of the priests. In the *Res Gestae* he claimed to have advanced as many as 170 candidates to various priesthoods. This must in fact have been a useful way in which to show appreciation for loyal support, as the major colleges of priests were still rather exclusive bodies, and membership remained a coveted social distinction.

While Augustus took steps to restore to their traditional strength the numbers of the various colleges of priests, he also introduced changes in the role of the colleges which had far-reaching effects. The great colleges were now scarcely involved at all in the process of political decision-making, as they had been under the Republic. It became a very rare occurrence for the taking of the auspices to be used to block an election, and consultation of the Sibylline Books, or of the *pontifices*, about political affairs declined. Instead, the colleges of priests were increasingly concerned with petitioning or thanking the gods on behalf of Augustus and his family, and this change in function accelerated under the emperors who came after Augustus. This can be seen in the case of the *fratres arvales* (Arval Brethren) some of whose records survive in the form of inscriptions. Originally the chief concern of this college was apparently with rites honouring the ancient Dea Dia to secure a good harvest, but rituals connected with the imperial family came to occupy the greater part of their time, after the college was revived by Augustus.

Games and sacrifices were held for the welfare of Augustus and other members of his family. The college of priests made offerings every year at the *Ara Pacis Augustae*. The vows traditionally made on 1 January for the safety of the state by the in-coming consuls were supplemented by vows made on 3 January for the safety of the emperor. These vows were at the same time taken by all the governors of the Roman provinces, so that this day became a time for intercession on behalf of the emperor throughout the Empire. Numerous anniversaries connected with Augustus and his family were marked by prayers; for example, prayers were offered on the anniversary of Augustus's first holding a magistracy (7 January), and on the anniversary of his receiving the title Augustus (16 January), and on his birthday. Succeeding emperors kept up this policy of marking anniversaries with religious festivals, so that eventually the Roman calendar was so cluttered with such occasions that a number of them had to be discontinued.

This shift in emphasis in the religion of Rome away from the state or

Left and below : Hadrian's Villa, the so-called Teatro Marittimo. Hadrian's most extravagant and ambitious building project was his villa near Tivoli, a huge complex of buildings, gardens and pools stretching for over a kilometre in length. The elegant apartments set on a little island, surrounded by a moat, edged by a colonnade, were probably the emperor's private quarters. Hadrian said that he intended to spend the last days of his life in this villa, devoting himself to painting, music and literature.

Hadrian's Villa, the Canopus. Parts of the vast complex of buildings were named after places which Hadrian had seen on his travels. This elongated pool seems to have represented the Canopus, a famous canal between Alexandria and Canopus in Egypt. Around the pool ran columns, some, as here at the north end, supporting arches alternating with straight lintels.

commonwealth to the person of the ruler or emperor marked a profound transformation in the nature of Roman state religion. The most important element in this radical change was the close association of the emperor with the gods, and the diffusion of emperor cults; in many rituals the emperor was in fact declared to be the son of a god, or even a god. On first consideration this belief, which flies in the face of common sense, appears bizarre, and it seems impossible that anyone seriously believed such a thing. In fact, in Rome itself with its Republican traditions, particularly among the senatorial aristocracy, with their interest in Greek philosophy, such an idea had met with strong resistance. Cicero had greatly objected to Julius Caesar's apparently aiming to secure recognition of himself as a god. Extravagant honours had been offered to Caesar, just as if he were a god, such as a gold throne in the Senate House and a ceremonial litter for carrying his statue in religious processions, a temple to his Clemency and a priest of his own cult. His statue was set up in one of the temples of Rome with the inscription 'To the Unconquered god', and the seventh month was renamed 'July' after him. Although these honours did not amount to the formal deification of Julius Caesar, yet, as Suetonius says, as a mere mortal he should certainly have refused them.

The Roman aristocracy undoubtedly found Julius Caesar's quasi-divine status offensive partly, if not chiefly, because in the ancient world divine status was closely connected with kingship, to which they were adamantly opposed. In the East there was a long tradition of divine rulers; the pharaohs of Egypt were god-kings, and the Hellenistic rulers of the kingdoms which were to become Rome's eastern provinces were traditionally honoured as gods.

Roman emperors were never formally deified during their lifetime, although in practice they were often accorded divine, or quasi-divine, status, particularly in the provinces; certainly Augustus was offered honours and forms of worship usually reserved for the gods. Augustus, and all the worthy emperors who came after him, were consecrated in Rome as gods after they died; Julius Caesar was, in fact, the first Roman in history to be recognized as a god in an official state cult after his death. At his funeral violent emotions were unleashed in the huge crowds attending the ceremony. The body was burnt in the Forum, and judges' chairs and benches from the law-courts were thrown onto the funeral pyre. The musicians and mourners who had walked in the funeral procession wearing robes which Caesar had worn at his Four Triumphs tore them off and flung them into the flames; veterans who had taken part in these triumphs added to the fire the arms which they had then carried. Women threw in their jewellery, together with gold buttons and embroidered tunics taken from their children. Snatching fire-brands from the funeral pyre, people ran off to try to burn down the houses of the conspirators Brutus and Cassius, who had been responsible for the murder of Caesar. Later, a marble column twenty feet high was raised to Caesar in the Forum, and people offered sacrifices at the foot of it, and made vows there, and settled disputes by oaths taken in the name of Caesar. The Senate formally decreed the deification of Caesar soon after his death, and added credibility was given to his divinity by the fact that on the first day of the Games given by his adopted son Octavian, later called Augustus, in honour of his apotheosis, a comet appeared about an hour before sunset, and shone for seven days. This was believed to be Caesar's soul elevated to Heaven. Virgil celebrated this event in a poem (*Eclogue* IX, 47–50, trans. E. V. Rieu):

> See how Olympian Caesar's star has climbed the sky,
> the star to gladden all our corn with grain
> and paint the grapes with purple on the sun-bathed hills.
> Graft your pears now, Daphnis;
> your children's children will enjoy the fruit.

Augustus's prestige was of course increased by the deification of Julius Caesar as he became 'son of god' (*divi filius*) as a result of it.

There was not in the ancient pagan world nearly so sharp a division between men and their gods as there came to be in Protestant Christianity. A number of long-revered gods, such as Hercules, Romulus, and Castor and Pollux, had, according to myth, been born mortals, and later been taken up into the company of the gods on account of their great deeds among men. Even in historical times the worship of popular heroes sometimes had sprung up spontaneously after their deaths; in the second century BC, after the murders of Tiberius and Gaius Gracchus, the popular reformers, statues were set up to them in Rome, and people came to sacrifice to and worship at these statues, as if at the shrines of gods. Among the Greeks the cult or worship of a great man after his death seems in special circumstances to have been entirely acceptable in the context of their religious beliefs; the founders of cities were regularly worshipped after their deaths as if they were divine, and the Hellenistic rulers of the Greek world who succeeded Alexander the Great acquired divine status and honours. In the Hellenistic world the giving of divine honours seems to have become a more or less conventional way of showing deep respect for particularly powerful people; in fact in time the Greeks came to offer divine honours to their Roman provincial governors. This is a situation which Antony appears to have exploited during his years in the eastern provinces of the Empire; according to Plutarch, he cavorted round Ephesus posing as the new Dionysus, or Bacchus, with women dressed as Bacchants and men and boys dressed like Satyrs and Pans to accompany

Overleaf: The edges of the Canopus were decorated with copies of famous Greek sculptures, including a row of caryatids, which are replicas of statues forming the Porch of the Maidens of the Erechtheum in Athens.

Above and opposite, below : Details of the Canopus, Hadrian's Villa.

Opposite, above : Detail of the statues decorating the Canopus.

him. The deification and worship of the Roman emperors involved the transfer of what had been private and unofficial rites, as in the case of the Gracchi, to the public sphere, and the adoption in Rome and the western part of the Empire of Hellenistic rituals and customs which accorded divine honours to the powerful. There has been a great deal of scholarly argument about precisely how the Romans and their subjects envisaged the divine status of the living emperor; was he classed as one of the gods, or was he only thought to have divine, or superhuman status? In fact during his lifetime an emperor's status was often, it appears, seen as being midway between that of god and man. A number of the prayers and sacrifices recorded as part of the worship of a living emperor were offered to the gods on behalf of the emperor, rather than to the emperor, so that although he was accorded divine honours and worship he was not treated exactly like a god. Sometimes sacrifices were offered directly to a living emperor, but here too a note of ambiguity about his precise status might creep in, being expressed perhaps in the type of victims offered. We should not really find this ambiguity about the emperor's divine status puzzling; it is scarcely surprising that there should have been some distinction between the status of the traditional gods and that of the emperor, or that people's views on so problematic a subject were not consistently and coherently formulated.

The idea of the Roman emperors' divinity was fashioned not so much by the policies of the emperors themselves, as by the apprehensive deference and abject submission of their subjects. The elevated status of the emperor was not simply imposed from above on unconcerned and indifferent subjects. His entourage and his humbler subjects co-operated to enhance his majestic status; being in no position to change or modify the existing power structure, they tended to pay homage to it, thereby ratifying their own place in the social order, and adding to their own self-esteem. They spontaneously lavished extravagant honours on the emperors, living and dead, in Rome and the provinces. Numerous statues of the emperors and of other members of their families were set up throughout the Empire, games were held in their honour, and temples and altars were erected to them. Indeed in the provinces the institution of the cult and worship of the emperor afforded an opportunity for the members of the local élite to safeguard and increase their own status by participating in an official capacity in the rites and observances of the cult. By taking part in the festivals and sacrifices honouring the emperor's birthday or other imperial anniversaries, and by assisting at dedication ceremonies, they emphasized their special relationship with the emperor and their association with his authority, while, at the same time, they communicated their loyalty, and that of their city or province, to the emperor.

A number of impressive monuments in Rome illustrate, or purport to illustrate, the process of deification and commemorate the deified emperors. Augustus built a temple to the deified Julius in the Roman Forum, of which parts survive, while Tiberius and Livia erected a temple to Divus Augustus (the Divine Augustus), of which something of the appearance is known from coins of Caligula celebrating its dedication, and from coins of Antoninus Pius commemorating its restoration, although no remains have been identified. When Hadrian himself rebuilt the Pantheon, which, according to the second century historian Dion Cassius, was originally erected by Agrippa in the time of Augustus, an image of Julius Caesar was included inside the building together with imagrs of Mars, Venus and other gods; there were statues of Augustus and of Agrippa, his loyal minister, in the porch of the temple, presumably set in the two great niches flanking the entrance to the rotunda. If this arrangement of statues goes back to the earlier building erected under Augustus, that building, in so far as it associated Augustus with the gods, obviously emphasized his nearness to the gods, and prepared the way for his eventual deification.

The curious rites of the actual ceremony of deification of a dead Roman emperor, as they were performed at some time during the second century AD, are preserved in an account given by the historian Herodian (4.2, trans.

C. R. Whittaker), who describes the proceedings as follows:

It is normal Roman practice to deify emperors who die. The body of the dead emperor is buried in the usual way with a very expensive funeral. But then they make a wax model exactly like the dead man and lay it on an enormous ivory couch at the entrance to the palace, and spread golden drapes under the effigy.

The model lies there pale like a sick man, and on either side of the couch people sit for most of the day. For seven days these ceremonies continue; each day the doctors come and go up to the couch, and each day they pretend to examine the patient and make an announcement that his condition is deteriorating. Then when it appears that he is dead, the noblest members of the equestrian order and picked young men from the senatorial order lift the couch up and take it out to the Campus Martius, where a square building made of vast wooden beams had been constructed in the shape of a house. Inside the building is completely filled with brushwood and outside it is decorated with gold-embroidered drapery, ivory carvings and with paintings.

The bier is taken up and placed on the second storey. Every perfume and incense on earth and all the aromatic herbs, fruits and juices are collected in great heaps. When an enormous heap of these aromatic spices has filled the entire space, a cavalry procession around the pyre begins; the whole equestrian order rides round and round in a circle in fixed formation, following the movement and rhythm of the Pyrrhic dance. Chariots circle round in the same formation carrying figures which wear masks of all the famous Roman generals and emperors.

When this part of the ceremony is over, the heir to the throne takes a torch and puts it to the built-up pyre. The whole structure easily catches fire because of the large amount of dry wood and of aromatic spices which have been piled high inside. Then from the topmost storey an eagle is released and soars up into the sky with the flames,

taking the soul of the emperor from earth to Heaven, as the Romans believe. After that he is worshipped with the rest of the gods.

Augustus himself, with the warning of Julius Caesar's fate before him, did what he could to avoid blatantly assuming divine status, particularly in Rome, during his lifetime. However, Augustus could not afford to suppress, or even ignore, all the divine honours which were offered to him; the use of religious ritual to express gratitude and loyalty to a ruler had become too entrenched in the current political system for it to be easily uprooted, and besides it was useful to Augustus. For the emperor came to serve as an indispensable focus for the loyalty and devotion of the inhabitants of the Roman Empire, and to be seen as the supreme symbol for the unity of that Empire. In every-day life there were constant reminders of the power and prestige of the emperors. There were portraits of the emperor on all the coins. Throughout the cities of the Empire statues of the emperor were set up in streets, squares and temples, often being dedicated by private citizens at their own expense. In fact, often the statue of the emperor was seen not simply as a monument, but as offering a refuge to those in trouble; in Rome slaves gained the right to flee to a statue of the emperor to complain of outrageous treatment.

In 2 BC the inhabitants of the city of Naples decided to set up games in his honour, and they dedicated a temple to him, the first temple in Italy dedicated to a living emperor. Lavish praise of Augustus honouring him as a god is recorded on inscriptions which were originally set up in public places in the cities of the eastern provinces of the Empire. Here is an example (now in the British Museum), which comes from Halicarnassus in Asia Minor:

Hadrian's villa. The colonnaded walk called 'Stoa Poikile', believed to be copied from the famous Stoa Poikile or painted portico at Athens, which was celebrated on account of its paintings of battle-scenes.

Immortal Nature, after overwhelming benefactions, has given mankind the greatest good of all, she has given us the emperor Augustus, who is not only Father of his country, Rome, and giver of happiness to our lives, but also the father, god and saviour of all mankind. It is he whose providence has not only fulfilled but even surpassed the prayers of all. For land and sea lie at peace, and the cities bloom with the flowers of order, concord and prosperity.

In the eastern provinces of the Empire, where there was a tradition of honouring rulers as gods, it would have been imprudent of Augustus to have refused divine honours since this might have undermined the loyalty of the provincials. To avoid seeming to assume directly divine status even in the eastern provinces, Augustus and his immediate successors usually permitted temples and cults to be set up in their honour only if they were associated with an established deity; very often this was the goddess Roma, the personification of the city, to whom there were already a number of altars and occasionally a temple in the east of the Empire, the worship of Roma having been established in Republican times in, for example, Rhodes, Delos, and Miletos. It is, in fact, engraved on the walls of the Temple of Rome and Augustus at Ancyra (Ankara) that the most complete version of the *Res Gestae* (Memoirs of Augustus) survives.

When Augustus allowed, or even encouraged, religious rituals in Rome and Italy which might appear to verge on worship of himself as a divinity, he was careful to see that they were not such as to revive the spectre of kingship. He appears rather to have tried to foster a sense of obligation and loyalty to himself by associating the Roman people to a certain extent in the rituals of his own family worship. For example, when Augustus revised the ancient festival of the Compitalia, at which in Republican times the guardian spirits (*Lares compitales*) had been worshipped at the intersections of the streets of the city of Rome in celebrations presided over by local leaders (*vicomagistri*), he added the cult of his Genius to that of the two spirits of the cross-roads, and the three spirits became known collectively as the *Lares Augusti*. The organization of this cult was the responsibility of freedmen, and they were assisted in the rituals by slaves, so this festival provided an opportunity for the people of Rome to demonstrate their loyalty to Augustus, and for the rich freedmen of the city to display their wealth and obtain some degree of social recognition. Ovid testifies to the previous decay of the worship of the spirits of the cross-roads, and to its revival by Augustus with the addition of the cult of his Genius, and says that there are now a thousand of these shrines in the city of Rome at which the three divinities are worshipped (*Fasti*, V, 134–6).

When, on the death of Lepidus, his former colleague as triumvir, Augustus was in 12 BC able to assume the office of high priest or *pontifex maximus* he did not move into the traditional residence of the high priest, but gave it to the Vestal Virgins. Augustus made part of his own house into a public shrine, displaying, as well as an image of the goddess Vesta and an ever-burning fire, the Lares and Penates of his own household. Thus the family worship of Augustus became a public cult in which the citizens of Rome were invited to take part, and Augustus's direction or headship of the state was made to appear to be under divine patronage.

While Augustus fostered loyalty to himself among the lower social classes at Rome by allowing his Genius to be associated with the celebration of the rites of the Compitalia, there appears to have been a parallel attempt to organize some sort of demonstration of loyalty among the upper classes in the city by the ruling that libations should be poured to his Genius at all public and private banquets. This was originally an honour voted to Augustus by decree of the Senate after his victory over Antony and Cleopatra, and was a clever extension of the cult of the Genius of the head of the household, which was part of the ordinary worship of Roman families. It was the custom for a man's friends to pay tribute to him on the occasion of his birthday by pouring libations to his Genius, so that the

Above: The Temple of Antoninus and Faustina, Rome, begun in AD 141, was originally dedicated by Antoninus Pius to his wife, who was accorded divine honours on her death. When Antoninus died in 161, the temple was dedicated to his memory as well, by decree of the Senate.

Below: Part of a marble relief apparently showing various measures taken by Trajan. The relief dates from the reign of Hadrian, and was found in the Forum. On this section, an emperor, perhaps Hadrian, addresses the people. Behind him is the Temple of the Deified Julius, to the left the Arch of Augustus.

offering of this honour to Augustus on a regular basis did not necessarily have to be interpreted as conferring divine status on him.

Finally, we may consider whether or not the inhabitants of the Roman Empire really did believe in the divinity of their emperor. A cynical interpretation of all the adulation lavished on him might be that men hoped to gain some advantage from it. In some, if not many, instances this may very well have been the case. However, we can never be sure whether the majority of the inhabitants of the Roman Empire believed that their emperor was a god, as we have no record of their opinions and beliefs. The surviving written evidence relates for the most part to the educated classes; we can only try to estimate what the views of the majority are likely to have been. In the time of Augustus the Roman Empire consisted of a number of different peoples of widely divergent cultural backgrounds, and among some of them it was already a well-established practice to honour their rulers as if they were gods; where this was the case, as in the eastern provinces which had formerly been the kingdoms of the Hellenistic successors of Alexander the Great, there would have been no difficulty about the acceptance of the divinity of the emperor. It is in those provinces of the empire that the most enthusiastic worship of Augustus as a god seems to have occurred; from the variety of divine honours offered to him it seems clear that for the most part they were something spontaneously proffered to the emperor, rather than imposed by Augustus or his agents.

It is more difficult to assess what is likely to have been the attitude of the majority of the inhabitants in the western provinces of the Empire; in these provinces the cult of the emperor was, in fact, sometimes instituted by the emperor's agents, rather than being initiated by the provincials themselves.

Among all classes in the Roman Empire, even among the educated élite, there appears to have been a high degree of credulity and superstition; for example, there was a widespread interest in astrology, in the casting of horoscopes and in magic of all kinds. It is not difficult to understand how, in such an atmosphere, many Romans would have been able to accept the idea of the emperor's divinity or superhuman status. The distinction between the natural and the supernatural, the human and the divine, was constantly blurred. We have seen how the Romans raised to divine status those mortals like Romulus and Hercules, who were felt to have rendered great services to mankind. There is no doubt that to the majority of Augustus's contemporaries, who had lived through the fighting and anarchy of the fifties and forties, he appeared as a saviour who had bestowed immeasurable benefits on men by the restoration of peace and order in the Roman world. Surrounded by feelings of such deep gratitude it was natural that Augustus should have come to be regarded as a god throughout the Empire. In spite of their fulsome rhetoric and obvious flattery, some sense of genuine gratitude to Augustus, and acknowledgment of his superhuman powers in restoring peace, comes through in inscriptions set up by the local officials throughout the east of the Empire.

The later years of the first century BC were a time of anxiety and uncertainty, when men began to question traditional beliefs. This was the beginning of a period when religious beliefs were in flux, when some rites might be abandoned, and others, like those connected with emperor worship, instituted in their place, although not without some degree of doubt and confusion. A curious story recounted by the historian Tacitus about the emperor Vespasian in AD 69, the first year of his reign, seems to capture something of the nature of the conflicting beliefs about the emperor's superhuman status. In his *Histories* (IV, 8) Tacitus wrote:

> There seemed to be signs that Vespasian enjoyed heaven's blessing and that the gods showed a certain partiality towards him. At Alexandria a poor man well known for his blindness threw himself at the emperor's feet, imploring him with groans to cure him of his blindness. He had been told to make this request by Serapis, the favourite god of a nation much addicted to strange beliefs. He begged Vespasian to

The Mausoleum of Hadrian, Rome. Constructed on the east bank of the Tiber, the Mausoleum was completed in AD 140. Hadrian also built the bridge, the Pons Aelius, which provides the approach to his Mausoleum. The huge stone drum, which contained the tomb-chamber, measures 210 feet in diameter, and was originally faced with marble. Converted into a fortress for the popes during the Middle Ages, this monument is now known as Castel S. Angelo.

Above : Painted panels forming a triptych with a portrait of a man flanked by representations of Serapis and Isis. This triptych may commemorate a family ancestor. The flanking representations of Serapis crowned by a gold modius, and Isis, with her characteristic headdress, are perhaps copies of well-known paintings of these gods displayed at one of their cult centres in Egypt. Vespasian and his sons were devotees of the Egyptian gods.

moisten his cheeks and eye-balls with his spit. A second petitioner, who had a withered hand, pleaded his case too, also on the advice of Serapis: would Caesar tread on him with his imperial foot?

At first Vespasian laughed and refused. When the two insisted he hesitated. At one moment he was alarmed by the thought he would be accused of vanity if he failed; at the next, the urgent appeals of the victims and the flattery of his entourage made him hope for success. Finally he asked the doctors for an opinion, whether blindness and atrophy of this sort were curable by human skill. The doctors discussed the matter from different points of view . . . a cure might be the will of the gods, and the emperor might be chosen to be the minister of divine will; at any rate all the credit for a cure would be the emperor's, whereas the ridicule for failure would fall on the sufferers. So Vespasian, supposing that all things were possible to his good fortune and that nothing was any longer past belief, smiling and surrounded by an expectant crowd of bystanders, accomplished what was asked. At once the cripple recovered the use of his hand, and the light of day dawned upon the blind man. Both these incidents are vouched for by people who were actually present, even now when nothing is to be gained by lying.

This story shows clearly the faith which ordinary people could feel in the superhuman powers of the emperor, and how belief in his divine status might arise. The emperor's position apart from and above that of other men is not seen as a pose cynically assumed by Vespasian to manipulate public opinion; rather it is thrust upon him by the attitudes of the crowd and the flattery of his immediate circle. At the same time, elements of doubt about the superhuman powers of the emperor are also reflected by this story; the doctors are plainly not sure what to think, and pompously prevaricate about the emperor's chances of curing the disabled. Vespasian, who has only recently been proclaimed emperor, at first feels unsure of himself, but comes to have faith in his own miraculous powers in response to the faith of those around him. Tacitus appears reluctant to believe in the miracles he describes, but is grudgingly convinced by the reports of eye-witnesses of the cures 'who now have nothing to gain by lying'. The fact that some educated people could doubt or question the super-human and quasi-divine powers of the emperor strongly suggests that others really did believe in them, however absurd such beliefs may seem in the modern rationalistic world.

Left : The approach to the Flavian Palace on the Palatine hill from the Forum, Rome. The huge palace was largely constructed by Domitian in the late first century AD. It remained the official residence of the emperors right down to late antiquity ; in fact our word 'palace' derives from it. Contemporaries were said to be astonished by the height of the rooms – they really felt the palace was the dwelling place of a ruler and a god.

81

PRIVATE LIFE AND PERSONAL RELIGION

We know relatively less about the private lives and personal religion of the Romans than about the state cults and organization of civic life, as of their very nature these things were, even in antiquity, largely hidden from view. The main sources from which we learn much of what we know about the state religion of Rome – the historians of political events, and the many official inscriptions and public buildings erected in connection with the state cults – do not, except in rare instances, illuminate the subject of private beliefs and religious practices. However, there are descriptions in Latin poetry of private religious ceremonies as well as of public ones, and there are the remains of small private shrines and of tombs, which, together with inscriptions related to them, tell us something about the personal religion of the ancient Romans.

The traditional religious rites practised by the Romans at home seem to have mirrored, although on a smaller scale, the rituals of the state religion. The main element of worship was the offering of sacrifice, while divination, particularly the consultation of *haruspices*, also played some part. As in public, so in private, religion regulated the structure and organization of much of the Romans' day-to-day life. The sentiments underlying private religious practices were similar to those underpinning the ceremonies conducted on behalf of the state; the emphasis was on propitiating the relevant gods and on obtaining their protection and co-operation in all the events and enterprises of everyday life. Stress was placed on the scrupulous discharge of all religious duties, rather than on moral behaviour as we would understand it.

A great deal of private religious ritual was centred round the Roman family; rites connected with such family events as births, marriages and deaths, were all more or less private ceremonies, usually organized by the head of the family, the *paterfamilias*. The Roman family was strongly patriarchal in character; a person's chief relationships were through the male line, although in time connections through the female line also came to be acknowledged, particularly if they could be exploited to increase a family's political influence. According to the laws of the Twelve Tables, the oldest formulation of Roman law, dating from the fifth century BC, the *paterfamilias* had absolute authority over all the members of his family and his household, even to the extent of having the power of life and death over them. (This right was eventually rescinded in the second century AD, and indeed we do not hear of it being exercised for a long period before that.) Sons remained in the power of their father even after they were grown up and married; legally they could not hold property in their own right unless they had been technically emancipated by their father, and we do not know how often this was done. Otherwise, only on the death of their father did they become fully independent, and at that time all the sons could expect an equal share of their father's estate. The only member of his

Fresco from the main hall of Livia's villa at Prima Porta, outside Rome. Livia, the wife of Augustus, owned this country villa, known as White Hen Villa, which was formerly decorated with mural frescoes representing a garden. The lush vegetation and bird perched on the low fence are realistically painted.

83

Right : Household shrine in the House of the Menander, Pompeii. In an exedra off the courtyard of this large house images of family ancestors, crudely represented in wood or wax, are displayed in a recess in the wall set behind an altar. The walls of the room are attractively painted with columns behind which rises a grove of trees, with birds perched among the branches.

Above : Shrine of the household gods in an atrium of the House of the Vetii, Pompeii, in the form of a niche framed by columns and a pediment, like a temple, within which the household gods are painted. In the centre stands the Genius, his head veiled appropriately for offering a sacrifice ; with his right hand he pours a libation. He is flanked by two Lares with drinking horns. A snake approaches to partake of the offerings ; it may be regarded as a symbol of fertility or as a personification of the Genius of the master of the house.

household over whom the *paterfamilias* might not have absolute control was his wife. Although according to the more old-fashioned form of marriage a wife passed from her father's power into that of her husband, by the newer form the wife remained under the legal control of her father, or of the guardian appointed by his will; this meant that she could have her own property, and that her husband could only avail himself of the income produced by her dowry. Fathers made the arrangements for their daughters' marriages, usually at so young an age that the girls were not likely to raise serious objections. For example, in the fourth century when Augustine at the age of thirty-one decided to give up his profligate life, a fiancée aged ten was found for him, although eventually he decided not to marry. Marriage was legal for a girl at twelve.

There is in Latin no exact equivalent for the word 'family' in the sense in which we most often use it as referring to the restricted 'nuclear' family of parents and children. The Latin word *familia* stands for the whole household of the *paterfamilias*, including his slaves, and his freedmen, together with his children and any other relatives living in the household. No doubt many households of free citizens did not own any slaves at all, while many others probably owned only a few. However, the households of the very rich often contained large numbers of slaves, as is indicated by the famous account of the millionaire Trimalchio's dinner-party by Petronius (first century AD). Trimalchio had slaves to accompany him to the public baths and play ball-games with him when he got there, while other slaves kept the score, and still others were detailed to retrieve the balls he dropped. Arrived at his house there was of course a door-keeper, and a steward to oversee the household. In the dining-room there were troupes of slaves to wait on his guests, who sang as they performed their duties, and took part in a series of practical jokes and hoaxes to amuse those at dinner. From the variety and quantity of food served it is obvious that there were several cooks in the kitchens, and slaves specializing in different types of carving were summoned to cut the portions of the variety of game which was served.

In fact as well as fiction huge households of slaves are recorded; when in AD 61 the City Prefect, a former consul, was murdered by one of his slaves, an ancient law whereby his whole household of slaves should be executed was enforced, although they numbered 400, including women and children. Since these slaves had not tried to prevent the murder of their master they were all held to be guilty – so great was the distrust of slaves among the Roman upper classes.

Every devout family, including the slaves, honoured its household gods (the Lares and Penates), the Genius or guardian spirit of the head of the family, the goddess of the hearth (Vesta), and probably also certain local gods.

The Lares and Penates seem to have been worshipped in very early times among the Romans. The Lares have been variously interpreted as either the spirits of the land, *i.e.* that of the farm, on which each individual Roman family depended in early times, or as the spirits of dead ancestors. The Penates were the spirits of the store cupboard. These gods were impersonal spirits, and, like all the old Roman gods, were without any mythology attached to them.

It was particularly with regard to the worship of the household gods that the very Roman virtue of *pietas* was most conspicuously exercised. *Pietas* may be translated 'duty' or 'loyalty'; it implied devotion both to the gods, and to one's parents and relatives. *Pius*, the adjective connected with *pietas*, meaning 'pious' or 'dutiful', is the word which Virgil chose to characterize Aeneas, the hero of his patriotic epic poem the *Aeneid*. Throughout Rome's long history the religion of family life appears to have persisted; the pious Roman respected his parents and relatives, and honoured his household gods in accordance with the customs of his ancestors.

Although we have no means of knowing how many Roman families in the last century of the Republic or in the early years of the Empire regularly worshipped their household gods, it is a striking fact that a large number of houses dating from these times have shrines for their household gods.

In Pompeii and Herculaneum, where so many of the precise details of everyday life have been preserved beneath the lava from the eruption of Vesuvius that covered the towns in AD 79, a number of the shrines of the household gods can still be seen in houses which have been excavated.

House of the Mosaic of Neptune and Amphitrite, Herculaneum. At the back of this house is a small courtyard forming an open-air dining-room. One wall is decorated with a mosaic plaque representing the sea-god Neptune and Amphitrite, his wife, beneath a large, shell-like motif. The house is named after this mosaic. The end wall is turned into a nymphaeum, or fountain, with a round-headed niche flanked by two smaller rectangular recesses, above which are hunting scenes with stags depicted in mosaic.

Funerary relief from Ostia of a child with a goat, perhaps a pet or else an animal for sacrifice. The inscription below includes a dedication to the spirits of the dead, who were widely believed to have supernatural powers. The child wears round his neck a bulla, or amulet, which was worn for protection until puberty.

These shrines, which vary in form, have been preserved in some cases with the images of the gods inside them, and are still decorated with paintings which illustrate the nature of the cult. In some of the houses at Pompeii, such as the House of Apollo, the shrine takes the form of a simple niche decorated with paintings, set in a wall of the kitchen, whereas in other houses the shrine takes the more elaborate form of an *aedicula*, or miniature temple, with small-scale columns and pediment, and is conspicuously placed against a wall of a colonnaded court or of the *atrium*.

Although in early times perhaps only one spirit or Lar was worshipped in each household, by the first century BC they seem to have been thought of as a pair, and at Pompeii they are always represented in paintings as a pair, usually being shown as young men wearing short tunics and holding drinking horns. In addition to having images of the guardian spirits of their household, devout Romans might also keep images of the particular deity or deities to whom they looked for protection. It appears that they were inclined to choose one particular 'patron' deity, for Plutarch (*c.* AD 50–*c.* 120) recounts that Sulla always carried an image of Apollo with him, and Apuleius (second century AD) says he always took an image of Mercury with him when he travelled. In the shrine of the household gods, in addition to the images, family mementoes and relics may also have been kept. In Petronius's story about the millionaire Trimalchio, the guests on entering the house see, in the portico decorated with frescoes of Trimalchio's life, the shrine of the household gods, in which is displayed, besides silver images of the Lares and a marble statuette of Venus, a gold casket in which they were told Trimalchio's first beard was kept.

Simple offerings were made to the guardian spirits, perhaps at every meal – offerings of cake, incense and wine. Thus in Petronius's story, towards the end of dinner, the images of Trimalchio's household gods are brought to the table by three slaves dressed in white, and one of the slaves prays for the favour of the gods whilst circulating a vessel for pouring libations of wine. The pig was the appropriate animal to sacrifice to the Lares.

With the worship of the Lares that of the Penates, or gods of the store cupboard, was closely associated; these were the spirits originally worshipped to ensure that each family had sufficient food. They too might be appeased with small offerings, such as the mixture of sacred flour and salt which might be thrown on the fire, or offered at the altar of the household gods.

The Genius, or special guardian spirit of the master of the house, was honoured in conjunction with the household gods. In the paintings decorating the household shrines, he is usually represented standing between the figures of the Lares. The origins of the cult of the Genius of the head of the family are obscure; it has been suggested that in early times the Genius was regarded as the life-force of the family, or the procreative power which enabled a family to continue from one generation to the next. However, by late Republican times the Genius was regarded as something much closer to a guardian spirit, or, as we might say, a guardian angel. A man's Genius was particularly honoured on his birthday by the pouring of libations. With the coming to power of Augustus it appears that the Genius of the emperor was also sometimes included among the spirits honoured at the household shrines, as in some shrines his Genius appears to be shown in the fresco paintings. In one of them it looks as though the figure of the Genius of Augustus was added to the existing picture of the Genius of the *paterfamilias* pouring a libation, with a note to explain that this was done when the Senate required it, that is, when it was decreed that a libation should be poured to Augustus at all private banquets.

There was, however, a darker and more sinister element in private religious customs than is found in the state rituals, at least in historical times; private individuals often had recourse to magical practices of various kinds, such as curses, incantations and spells. These practices reveal a crude and vicious streak in the mentality of the Romans, which was not

otherwise shown in their traditional religious customs. The most disgusting ingredients might be used in spells to bring harm or death to someone. For example, the historian Tacitus recounts that when Germanicus, Tiberius's adopted son, was dying from a mysterious illness in Antioch, he believed not only that he had been poisoned by Piso, the governor of the province who was his personal enemy, but also that Piso was hastening his death by magic. So Germanicus had his room searched, and according to Tacitus's account (*Annals*, II, 69):

> Examination of the floor and walls of his bedroom revealed the remains of human bodies, spells, curses, lead tablets inscribed with the name Germanicus, human remains snatched half-burnt from the pyre and besmirched with putrid gore, and other objects with the power to bewitch, by means of which it is believed that souls are given over to the powers of the underworld.

Magic was practised at all levels of society from peasants to emperors; in the early years of the Empire accusations of sorcery were quite a common feature of the charges brought against members of the senatorial class on trial for treason. The emperor Nero apparently had recourse to magicians; tormented with guilt at having arranged the murder of his mother he tried to call up her spirit so that he could beg her forgiveness.

Magic primarily consists of a combination of occult words and rites designed to influence the course of nature. In the Graeco-Roman world magic was far less clearly separated from religion, with its emphasis on the correct performance of ritual, than it has become in the very different

Stucco decoration from the ceiling of a house of late Republican date in Rome. The fertility god Priapus is represented among the figures shown against a background of shrines in the countryside.

87

Tombs beyond the walls of Pompeii. In the background is the volcano Vesuvius, which erupted in AD 79, burying Pompeii and Herculaneum beneath a layer of lava which preserved their remains for posterity. Pliny described the cloud of smoke and ashes which rose from the summit as 'like an umbrella pine, as it rose high on a sort of trunk, and split off into branches'.

religious climate of Christianity. But some distinctions can be made; magical practices implied an element of compulsion – if the correct procedure was precisely carried out, the desired result was bound to follow, whereas in religious rites the Romans sought rather to win over and propitiate the supernatural powers by persuasive prayers and sacrifices. However, there was a considerable degree of overlap between religion and magic; in magical observances, invocations to the gods as well as elements of sacred rituals were borrowed from traditional religious customs. Many magic rites invoked the deities of the underworld, and required the assistance of ghosts. The celebration of such rites usually took place in sordid circumstances, with uncouth assistants, and aided by the magic properties of frequently repulsive objects, like those human remains used to bewitch Germanicus.

Since in the ancient world a considerable part of everyday life was attended by ritual words and acts, it is often difficult to know where to draw the line between religious and magical practices; for example, Augustus is said always to have carried an amulet of seal-skin as a protection against thunder and lightning, while Julius Caesar repeated a spell three times whenever he entered a carriage so as to ensure a safe journey. Such superstitious practices seem closer to magic than to religion. To some extent the Romans seem to have distinguished between acceptable religious rites and unacceptable magic ones on moral grounds – depending on whether the objective in view was good or bad, honourable or shameful. Rites intended to ensure good crops or to cure illness were acceptable, whereas a provision of the law of the Twelve Tables forbade the bewitching of the neighbour's crops. Within the sphere of religion fell all those things which might be prayed for openly in temple precincts, such as health, prosperity, or a child, while less reputable needs and wishes were the province of magic – making or breaking an erotic tie, a cure for impotence, a win in the chariot races, or revenge for injuries suffered. Curses dealing with such matters, inscribed on lead tablets, have been discovered in considerable numbers in widely separated parts of the Roman empire, such as northern Africa, Asia Minor, and Britain. One such inscribed curse (in H. Dessau, *Inscriptiones Latinae Selectae*, 8753) from northern Africa relates to chariot-racing. It begins:

> I invoke you Demon, whoever you are, and lay it upon you from this hour, this day, this moment that you torment and destroy the horses of the Greens and the Whites, kill and crush the charioteers Clarus, Felix, Primulus and Romanus, leave no breath in their bodies.

Lead tablets inscribed with curses were often buried in graves so as to enlist the help of the ghost of the dead person. The magic formulae used in the Latin examples are largely derived from Greek curses, so it appears that this type of magic was imported from the Hellenistic world. Sometimes these curse tablets have been found buried together with figurines representing mutilated persons; or the figurines have their arms and legs bound, or are transfixed by bronze nails through the heart or stomach. These curses might invoke obscure, non-Roman gods or unknown spirits, or the powers of the underworld. Similarly, according to descriptions preserved in some Latin poems, the witches often call on Hecate or Pluto, Greek deities of the underworld, as they go about preparing love-philtres and spells. Horace (*Satires*, I, viii, 23–34) gives a lurid description of two witches practising magic, as recounted by the fertility god Priapus:

> I have seen with my own eyes Canidia coming, with her black dress tucked up, her feet bare, and her hair loose, together with Sagana, her elder, shrieking. Their pallid complexions made them terrifying to look at. They began by scratching up the earth with their nails and tearing apart a young ewe lamb with their teeth. The blood drained into a trench so that thereupon they might summon up the shades of

the dead to practise necromancy. There was an effigy of wool, and another of wax; the woollen one was the larger, to restrain the smaller for punishment. The wax image stood submissively, as if doomed to a slave's death. One witch called on Hecate, the other on cruel Tisiphone.

Eventually Priapus farts so loudly in his terror at these goings-on, that the witches, now frightened themselves, run off. Obviously this is exaggerated literary horror, and should not be taken too seriously, but the magic rites practised by Horace's witches undoubtedly derive from procedures that were actually carried out. Virgil (*Eclogue*, VIII, 73–82) describes the magic used by a woman to draw her lover to her, and these rites seem to reflect the practices which really were used. This poem is modelled on a Greek one by Theocritus:

> Draw Daphnis home from the city, my spells, draw him home. I bind you with three threads of three different colours and I take the image three times round the altar. The god delights in odd numbers. Draw Daphnis home from the city, my spells, draw him home. Twine three colours into three knots, Amaryllis, twine them and say 'I am binding chains of love'. Draw Daphnis home from the city, my spells, draw him home. As this clay grows hard and this wax melts in one and the same fire, so may my love of Daphnis be – softening him to me, and hardening him to others.

Until the last years of the Republic we hear almost nothing of the practice of magic arts in the higher strata of Roman society, but things were changing, at first slowly, and then during the early years of the Empire at an accelerated pace. During the first and second centuries AD magic became much more prevalent in Roman society than it had been hitherto; this may have been due in part to the introduction into Rome from the East of a new kind of learned magic allegedly based on the wisdom of Persia, and going back to the great magus Zoroaster. Elements of this form of magic, its doctrines and incantations, are preserved in Egyptian papyri, and they show the influence of Greek, Jewish and Egyptian occult beliefs. In part, however, we may assume that the previously more or less un-noticed forms of traditional magic which had been practised by the uneducated from time immemorial invaded classes of society that had formerly been immune to such superstitions. In the period of the late Republic a number of prominent senators are known to have dabbled in magic. The learned and otherwise respectable P. Nigidius Figulus was influential at Rome in spreading the revival of Pythagorean beliefs in immortality and the transmigration of souls, but Pythagoreanism included numerous magical elements, and its adherents were accused of practising forbidden and sacrilegious arts. It was said that among their abominable rites they sacrificed children and sought to raise the dead. Appius Claudius Pulcher, who was consul in 54 BC, was also believed to practise necromancy.

Under the early Empire allegations that members of the upper classes were practising magic became more frequent. A number of hypotheses have been advanced to explain the increase in the number of accusations to do with the practice of magic among the élite. It has been suggested that rebels and conspirators are found in many periods of history to have consulted diviners and seers about their chances of success, and that it was this aspect of magic which frightened the Roman emperors and led to prosecutions. For it was believed in Roman times that by magic means knowledge of the future might be obtained, and such foreknowledge might have encouraged conspirators to proceed with their plots – or so the emperors may have feared. A very different explanation has been suggested, deriving from the observation that accusations of sorcery are particularly likely to occur 'when two systems of power are sensed to clash within the one society' (P. Brown, *Religion and Society in the Age of St Augustine*, 124). Certainly there was this type of power struggle in the early years

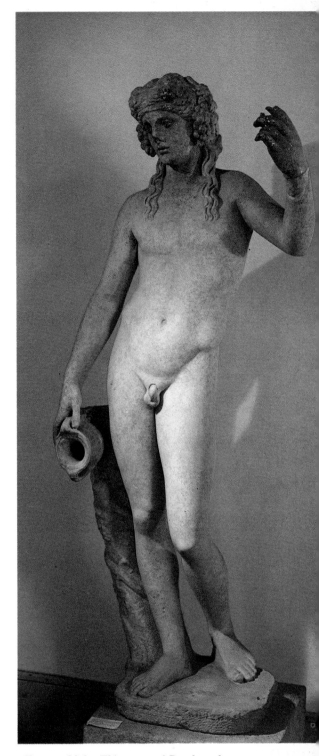

Above and left : This statue of Bacchus, the youthful god of wine, comes from the Sanctuary dedicated to the Syrian gods on the Janiculum hill in Rome. It is a copy of a Hellenistic statue of the Greek god Dionysus with whom the Roman god Bacchus was assimilated. Dionysus was believed to have come from the East.

of the Empire – the conflict between, on the one hand, the descendants of the former ruling classes – the senatorial families, and on the other the relatively newly established emperors and their entourage. From the early years of the Empire onwards magic began to intrude into public life. In the second century AD the emperor himself resorted to sorcery to aid him in military affairs; the story is told that even Marcus Aurelius became the dupe of the false prophet Alexander of Abonoteichus. This charlatan held court delivering bogus oracles with the aid of an obliging snake named Glycon, whom he had fitted out with an artificial snake's head of linen, anthropomorphic in appearance, painted and very life-like, which would open and close its mouth by the use of a horsehair, and which had a forked black tongue, like a snake's darting out, also moved by hairs. Alexander himself was a striking figure, who would put on a show of madness, foaming at the mouth. This he achieved by chewing soapwort, a plant used in dyeing, but the spectators thought the foam an awe-inspiring visitation. (Lucian, *Alexander*, 12 ff.) On the advice of this man Marcus Aurelius had two lions and a load of costly unguents thrown into the river Danube before engaging in a battle. Hardly surprisingly, the lions swam to the river bank and the Romans were defeated.

By the second century AD the validity of magic was widely accepted. Apuleius the writer, who was a native of north Africa, had to defend himself at Sabratha in AD 158–9 against a prosecution for practising magic. Accused of using magic arts to entice a rich widow to marry him, he rebutted the charges but did not deny the possibility of magic. Far from it – part of the speech he made in his defence runs as follows (*Apology*, 26):

> You who so lightly bring charges against magic, do you realize that it is an art blessed by the immortal gods, well versed in worship and adoration, religious of course, and with an intimate knowledge of the divine; it has been honoured from the time of its originators, Zoroaster and Oromasdes, as the high priestess of the powers of heaven.

Apuleius, like many others of his time, considered that magic was carried out by the agency of demons, who were conceived of as intermediate between the gods and men. The precise nature of these demons, or spirits, who might be invoked in curses or spells, or who might otherwise harm the living, does not emerge clearly in any account which has come down to us from this period of antiquity. This is scarcely surprising as the realm of these spirits was that of 'the shadowy, the shameful, the illegal and the illiterate' (see R. MacMullen, *Paganism in the Roman Empire*). However, most Romans appear to have believed in them.

Although they played no part in the official state cults of Rome, dreams were undoubtedly important in the private religious lives of the Romans. Most Romans were extraordinarily apprehensive about the future, and dreams were often regarded as prophetic. Suetonius recounts (*Augustus*, 91) that before the Battle of Philippi:

> Augustus . . . when so ill that he decided not to leave his tent, changed his mind on account of a friend's dream – most fortunately too as it proved. The camp was captured, and a party of enemy breaking into the tent, plunged their swords through and through his bed, thinking he was still in it, cutting the bed-clothes to ribbons.

Dreams played an important part in the miraculous cures from illness which numerous people sought at the great sanctuaries of Asclepius at Epidaurus in Greece and Pergamon in Asia Minor. Asclepius, who was in origin a Greek hero – during his life a renowned physician – but elevated early on to the status of full divinity, was in Greek times chiefly worshipped at the sanctuary at Epidaurus. The sick flocked there, to spend the night in his temple where it was believed that the god would appear to them in a vision as they slept, and prescribe what they should do to be restored to

*Pompeii, Street of the Tombs, beyond the
Herculaneum Gate. The tombs of Pompeii, like
those of Rome, were placed close together along
the sides of the roads beyond the city gates. Burial
inside the city was forbidden, as it had been from
early times within the city of Rome.*

Above and opposite : Tombs in the Isola Sacra Cemetery near Ostia. This cemetery was largely used by small traders and craftsmen, who are buried in the many rectangular-shaped barrel-vaulted tombs. No place for slaves was made in these family tombs. Their graves are marked by the necks of large broken jars sticking up out of the ground. The ashes of the dead were buried beneath these broken jars, through the necks of which libations were poured.

health; or they simply awoke cured. Many dedications and ex-votos bear witness to the popularity of the cult and the miraculous cures achieved. At the command of the Sibylline Books this cult was imported to Rome in the early third century BC during a plague, and a temple housing the image of the god and his sacred snake was established on the Tiber Island. This, however, was not one of the great centres of healing; rather there are records of many Romans, together with numerous inhabitants of the east of the Empire travelling to the Sanctuary of Asclepius at Pergamon to seek remedies for their illnesses from the god, who would appear to them while they slept in his sanctuary. It was during the second century AD that the worship of Asclepius at Pergamon attained its greatest popularity. The cult of Asclepius allowed for a much more personal relationship between the deity and the worshipper than is found in the state religion. In some ways the cult of Asclepius afforded to his worshippers a religious experience similar to that provided by the mystery religions for their initiates – a feeling of closeness to the deity and the stimulation of ardent devotion to his cult.

All the important stages of life – birth, puberty, marriage and death – were marked by religious ceremonies. Childbirth was an exceedingly hazardous process, and infant mortality was enormously high throughout the Roman period, so it is scarcely surprising to find that the birth of a child was the occasion for a number of religious rites. A table was set out in the *atrium*, or main hall of the house, for Juno Lucina, the goddess of childbirth, and it remained there until the child was named, eight days after birth if the child was a girl, and nine if it was a boy. At least in early times the evil spirits of the countryside were kept from entering a house where there was a new-born child by three men with an axe, a broom and a club coming at night to beat the threshold of the house.

The occasion of a boy reaching puberty around the age of fourteen was also a time for rites and ceremonies, although these might be postponed until he was fifteen or sixteen. First he took off the gold *bulla* or amulet which he had worn round his neck for protection throughout childhood and dedicated it to the household gods. Then he took off the striped toga worn by free-born children, and assumed for the first time the plain toga worn by men. Sacrifices were offered to the gods, the youth was escorted to the forum, and his name was enrolled on the official list of citizens, in the *tabularium*, or record office. These occasions were attended by family friends, very much in the way that weddings and betrothal parties were attended, for rich families appear to have given a dinner and reception as part of the celebrations. This 'coming-of-age' ceremony was usually, although not invariably, held on 17 March, the festival of Liber Pater, an Italian god of fertility and wine, who was assimilated with the Greek god Dionysus, and whose festival was obviously an appropriate time for feasting and drinking. After this ceremony the sons of senators were encouraged to attend meetings of the Senate as spectators, and to familiarize themselves with aspects of public life and administration before entering on a period of military service. A young man did not at this time gain full control of his property and of his financial interests even if his father had already died; a trustee or guardian for his financial affairs was selected to assist him until he reached the age of twenty-five.

At puberty a girl devoted her toys and the striped toga she had worn as a child to the household gods. From the examination of a number of funerary inscriptions of Roman women which state the age at which they were wed, it appears that around a quarter of them married before reaching the age of fourteen. A girl might, however, be betrothed or engaged when only ten years old. In these circumstances it is hardly surprising that the betrothal ceremony was not legally binding. The betrothal was marked by a ceremony and the exchange of gifts between the girl and her fiancé; these usually included the gift of a ring, often of gold, from the young man to the girl. This she placed on the fourth finger of her left hand, as is still the custom today.

As in many societies, even modern ones, marriage was marked by a mixture of religious rites and ceremonies and superstitious customs. Marriage was a central institution of Roman society as the family formed the basic unit of that society; regularized and legitimate marriages were required to produce legitimate children to become the next generation of citizens, and to be the legal heirs of their father's property. Hence there were some restrictions on marriage; a Roman citizen could not marry a non-citizen, and members of the highest, senatorial, class, could not marry former slaves. At first by custom, and later by law, members of the senatorial class were debarred from marrying actresses.

Marriages were not usually solemnized in Rome during May, probably because this was the month when the ghosts of the dead were believed to be especially close to the living, and when the festival and rituals of the Lemuria were celebrated to appease them. The first half of June, until the rites in honour of Vesta were completed on June 15, also seems to have been considered an unlucky time to get married. Since there are many references in Latin literature to the customs and religious rituals pertaining to the Roman marriage ceremony, it is possible to reconstruct in considerable detail how a wedding was celebrated in ancient Rome. On her wedding-day the bride wore a long white robe with a woollen girdle round her waist

Tomb in the Isola Sacra cemetery, embellished with a stone carving of a flower.

fastened in a double knot called a Hercules knot. Over her face and her hair, which had been elaborately dressed in the fashion of the Vestal Virgins, she put the bridal veil, which was traditionally of a flaming red or orange colour. A wreath of flowers was then placed on top of her veiled head. The bridegroom, his family and friends came to the house of the bride and the two families together offered a sacrifice, usually a pig but sometimes a ewe, either in some nearby temple or in the *atrium* of the house itself. In early times at least, a specially appointed augur, or seer, consulted the omens to see if the gods favoured the marriage. However, Cicero tells us that by his time the presence of a seer was just a formality. The marriage contract was signed and witnessed by a number of the guests, usually ten, and the couple joined their right hands and exchanged vows. Feasting until night-fall followed and then a procession was formed to escort the bride from her father's house to that of her husband. Torch-bearers and sometimes flute-players led the way, and the guests joined in the procession, singing ribald songs and throwing nuts. When the bride reached her new house she was carried across the threshold lest she should stumble over it, which would have been a bad omen. Inside the house an elderly woman called the *pronuba*, whom, it was stipulated, should have had only one husband, led the bride to the marriage-bed, which was set out in the *atrium* of the house, or in an adjoining room. The bride's attendants and the rest of the party then withdrew, leaving the couple alone to consummate the marriage.

Although provision for divorce was made even in early times, the dissolution of a marriage seems to have been a rare occurrence until the later years of the second century BC. However, in the last years of the Republic, divorce became so frequent that it was thought to threaten the stability of family life. In the same period family life was even more seriously threatened by a decline in the birth rate; during the last century of the Republic and the first centuries of the Empire many upper-class Roman families died out. We do not know whether this trend was also matched among the poor, as we lack comparable evidence. Numerous explanations for these facts have been put forward; the increasing emancipation of women has been blamed on the grounds that women who remained independent of their husbands and in control of their own property, and who changed their husbands apparently at whim, or for financial gain, were reluctant to undergo the hazards of childbirth. Seneca complains of the aristocratic women who reckoned the year not by the names of the consuls, which was the normal method in Rome, but by the names of their husbands. 'They divorce in order to re-marry. They marry in order to divorce.' The high incidence of infant and child mortality, miscarriage, contraception and infertility have also been advanced as reasons for the declining birth-rate and dying-out of old families. These are all areas in which evidence is difficult to obtain, so the various theories put forward remain largely speculative. It has also been suggested that the apparent failure of the Romans to produce large families was due to chronic lead poisoning, leading to infertility. The water which they drank ran through lead pipes, and many of the pots used for cooking were made of lead; a number of skeletons which have been analyzed have shown an abnormally high lead content. Certainly the high rate of infant and child mortality accounted in part for the small size of families, and in some cases for their extinction. The emperor Marcus Aurelius and his wife Faustina had thirteen children of whom only three lived to grow up and marry. In the 600 funerary inscriptions found at Ostia on which the age at death of the person commemorated is recorded, almost half died before the age of five.

In 18 BC Augustus introduced legislation in an attempt both to stem the tide of scandalous divorces, and to encourage married couples to have more children. Adultery was no longer considered a private offence but a serious crime, which could result in a guilty wife and her lover being exiled from Rome, and in the confiscation of a large part of their property. Women who were mothers of three or more children were freed from their guardians, while their husbands were granted more rapid promotion in the senatorial

to be wasted. In another *Letter* (VIII, 8) he writes of his own visit to a revered and celebrated country site at the source of the River Clitumnus, near Trevi (Trebiae) in Umbria. He describes the springs which form the source of the river rising in a dark grove of cypress trees, and the river itself with its water as cold and as white as snow. Pliny continues:

Left and above : The Great Ludovisi Sarcophagus, ornately carved in marble, depicting a battle scene. This sarcophagus, which dates from the mid-third century AD, may be that of Hostilian, one of the sons of the emperor Decius. A general on a prancing horse presides over the struggle between the Roman soldiers and shaggy barbarians locked in mortal combat.

> Nearby is a holy temple of great antiquity, with the god Clitumnus himself standing there wearing a robe with a purple border. The oracular shrines around bear witness that his divinity is present and that it has the power of prophecy. There is a large number of other shrines scattered around the site, each for a different god, each of whom has his own title and his own ceremonies, and even his own spring. . . . You will also find something worth studying here, for you will read many inscriptions by large numbers of people all over the columns and walls of the temple, in praise of the spring and its god. Many of these you will admire, but some you will laugh at; but no – you in fact are too kindhearted to laugh at any of them.

There is no reason to infer from the last sentence of the letter, in which Pliny scoffs at the no doubt simple-minded devotion of some of the worshippers at the temple, that Pliny wished to discredit the religious associations of this place; the whole tenor of his letter, with its evocative description of the sacred place, is against such an interpretation. Today there still stands near the sacred springs an early Christian church, probably of the fifth century AD, which is largely constructed of the remains of earlier classical buildings. Most probably these antique columns and other architectural fragments now incorporated in the church were taken from the shrines and temple which stood by the river and its source in pagan times. The replacing or transformation of the pagan shrine into a Christian church provides a vivid example of the way early Christianity took over revered pagan sites, and of the long tradition of worship in such hallowed places.

THE MYSTERY RELIGIONS

The state cults of gods like Jupiter and Mars and the religious rites such as the worship of household gods constituted the religion which was peculiarly and uniquely Roman. There were, however, other important and influential cults, quite distinct from the traditional beliefs and forms of worship, which infiltrated the Roman world from the East over a long period of time. These were the mystery religions, or oriental cults, as they are sometimes called. Among them were the worship of Isis, which came from Egypt, the cult of Mithras which came from Iran, the worship of the Great Mother-goddess Cybele from Asia Minor, and the Mysteries of Dionysus, or Bacchus, which came from Greece.

The worship of the gods of the mystery cults involved initiation ceremonies for their devotees and secret, often orgiastic, rites; Roman moralists complained that these cults gave scope for all kinds of licentious activity under the cover of religion. No doubt what particularly aroused their suspicions was that the cults were especially popular with women, and moreover their rituals were often celebrated at night. At a more fundamental level the cults might be regarded as objectionable because, with the partial exception of that of Cybele, they were not concerned with fostering the success and prosperity of the Roman state, which was the object of the traditional religious cults. Rather, the mystery religions were concerned with the salvation of the individual and with his personal relationship with the deity, and their ceremonies powerfully engaged the emotions of their devotees. Among the Romans, membership of these religious groups was not acquired by birth, as was the obligation to pay homage to the state gods. The worship of the gods of the mystery cults was instead a matter for personal choice and conviction. Eventually adherence to these cults cut across the old national and racial boundaries – their votaries might include humble inhabitants of Egypt and Asia Minor as well as Roman citizens, and most of the mystery cults were open to despised sections of society, such as women and slaves, while many of the rites celebrating the gods of the Roman state were not.

Thus, in the early years of the Empire, any Roman town, and indeed Rome itself, presented a bewildering variety of religious edifices to view. At Ostia, for example, in addition to the conventional temples of the state gods such as the Capitolium and Temple of Hercules, and the shrines or altars set up to spirits like Silvanus or the Nymphs, there were at least fifteen shrines, or Mithraea, built for the worship of Mithras, and a large area was set aside for the worship of Cybele, with a temple to her, a shrine to her consort Attis, and guild houses for the associations of men who took part in her cult processions.

The variety of religious beliefs held in the Roman world, particularly under the Empire, was to a considerable extent the result of the huge influx of foreigners into the previously more or less homogeneous societies

Above : Relief with gladiators, found on the Appian Way outside Rome.

Right : The substructure of the amphitheatre at Pozzuoli.

Fresco in the Villa of the Mysteries, Pompeii, showing an Egyptian deity crouching. It is perhaps Horus.

of Rome and the rest of Italy. These immigrants brought with them religious beliefs and practices quite different from those of Rome, and their exotic cults caught on, and gradually gained adherents among the established population of Rome and Italy. The satirist Juvenal complains bitterly of the infiltration of a motley crowd of aliens into Rome, and of the pollution of the River Tiber by muddy floods of superstition pouring in from the Syrian river, Orontes. Tacitus has a senator, Cassius Longinus, denouce, for similar reasons, the huge households of slaves of foreign origin common in his time. These were, he said, 'subject to different religious sanctions from those of their masters – or to none at all'.

In spite of such prejudices, the ancient Roman world, in so far as it harboured a number of quite separate religious sects and systems of belief, enjoyed an unprecedented degree of religious toleration. There were, however, some notable exceptions to this general principle; the Jews and Christians were suppressed intermittently, and Druids permanently. Nevertheless, until Christianity became the official religion of the Empire, there was, in general, widespread toleration of religious beliefs and cults imported to Rome and Italy from the East. Over the centuries there were of course some instances of restriction and restraint. Roman citizens were forbidden to take part in the orgiastic rites of the cult of Cybele in the Republican period, while in 186 BC the Senate passed a decree aimed at repressing the rites in honour of Bacchus on account of the disorderly conduct of the worshippers.

The most important and significant limitation on religious toleration was with regard to the adherents of Christianity. The causes of the persecutions of the Christians seem to have been various. Christians are first mentioned in Roman historical writing by Tacitus. While he refers to them disparagingly as the adherents of a pernicious superstition, he also says that Nero made them scapegoats for the great fire of Rome in AD 64, in order to divert suspicion from himself as the instigator of the fire. Under Nero's direction the Christians were persecuted with hideous cruelty: '. . . dressed in wild animals' skins they were torn to pieces by dogs, or made into torches to be lit up after dark' (Tacitus, *Annals*, XV, 44). Later on Christians were persecuted because they did not worship the Roman gods and did not offer sacrifice for the emperors; there were widespread fears that the neglect of the pagan gods by the Christians would endanger the peace of the gods and so be a cause of damage and disaster to the Roman state. Christians, unlike the adherents of other religious sects in the Roman world with the exception of the Jews, claimed to have the only true religion, attacking the honours offered to the pagan gods. Therefore with the rise of Christianity to a dominant position in the Empire the benefit of religious toleration was to disappear for many centuries from the Western world.

The great rise in popularity of the mystery religions under the Empire used often to be attributed to the revulsion of high-minded people from the increasing decadence of the times, and to the weakening of traditional religious beliefs. Carcopino wrote that the Roman pantheon still persisted, 'but that the spirits of men had fled from the old religion; it still commanded their service, but no longer their hearts or their belief'. There does not seem to be any evidence for this interpretation. The traditional polytheistic religion appears to have retained its importance and its credibility until well on into the third century, if not beyond; dedicatory inscriptions and newly built or repaired temples testify to this. The fact that Christian writers, like Augustine, devoted much of their time to attacking the old pagan gods shows that they were still a potent force with which to reckon. In fact, it appears that the mystery cults, with the exception of that of Mithras, largely died out earlier than did the worship of the traditional gods of the state; the Eastern cults enjoyed their widest popularity in the time of the Antonine and Severan emperors, and then began to decline. Across the Empire the cults of the principal Roman deities, Jupiter, Mars and Hercules, remained the most important; for example, theirs were the images which appeared most frequently on the imperial coinage.

We know that when members of the imperial family became initiates of a particular mystery cult they continued to worship the gods of the state, and no doubt other people did the same. Augustus was an initiate of the Eleusinian Mysteries, while Vespasian and his sons were devotees of the Egyptian gods, Isis and Serapis. In the second century AD, emperor Antoninus Pius and his wife Faustina were devotees of the cult of Cybele. There is in fact no reason to suppose that the cult of Isis, or indeed any of the other mystery cults, dispensed their worshippers from existing religious obligations either to the gods of the state or to their household gods.

The assertion that it was the increasing decadence of the times that gave rise to the vogue for the mystery cults can also be questioned. Although it is something of a commonplace for men to disparage their own times, and to look back with nostalgia to some earlier and nobler epoch, there were well-founded reasons for seeing the onset of imperial rule as a period of

Below left and below : A relief found at Ariccia, south of Rome, which illustrates the celebration of religious rites in Egypt, identified by the ibises. The cult was probably connected with Isis. To the right, on a platform, worshippers gesticulate in time to music while in the centre dancers, both male and female, cavort in a frenzy. Such dancers were nicknamed 'wagtails' in Greek.

decay for the time-honoured way of life of at least some sections of Roman society. In particular the coming of the Empire deprived the old senatorial governing class of its political power, and even of its personal liberty. The system of government inaugurated with the principate of Augustus, which was in reality monarchical, though it operated behind the façade of the old republican forms of government, was degrading and demoralizing to the former ruling classes, since it demanded of them insincere and inconsistent behaviour. Tacitus brings this out clearly when he describes their reactions and conduct on hearing of the death of Augustus and the accession of Tiberius (*Annals*, I, 7):

> At Rome, consuls, senate, knights rushed headlong into slavery. The greater a man was, the greater the insincerity and haste. They must show neither happiness at the death of one emperor, nor too much grief at the accession of the next: so their features were carefully arranged in a blend of tears and smiles, mourning and flattery.

However, deprived of their traditional role in life by political changes, members of the former governing classes turned not to the mystery cults for a new ideology to support and regulate their lives, but to the tenets of Stoic philosophy, which had originated in Athens. Stoicism, with its emphasis on morality and virtue, gave men something to live for – moral self-respect – and argued that the universe was divinely ordered for the benefit of mankind. The Stoic endeavoured to lead a good life, following the sect's beliefs about the nature of good and evil; as the Stoic emperor Marcus Aurelius wrote, 'Nothing is for a man's good, except what makes him just, temperate, brave and free' (*Meditations*, VIII, 14). At the same time, the Stoic teaching that a man should be guided by his own judgement of what was right, and not yield to any external authority, on occasion hardened men's resolution to resist the unjust tyranny of an emperor. 'If a man can look at flashing swords with eyes unswerving, if he knows that it is of no importance to him whether his soul departs through mouth or throat, call him happy,' wrote Seneca, the well-known Stoic philosopher, who courageously killed himself during the time of Nero.

It is notoriously difficult to assess 'decadence' in any society; certainly there is plenty of evidence in the Rome of the late first century BC and the first century AD of changing, if not declining, moral standards in private life. Rich and poor both enjoyed the revolting spectacles of the amphitheatres of Rome, in which thousands of wild animals, conscripted gladiators, condemned criminals of both sexes, and prisoners of war were 'butcher'd to make a Roman holiday' (Byron, *Childe Harold*). The staleness of repetition could be avoided only by an escalation in the quantity of the victims involved and the degree of brutality employed. Under the Empire there was a steady progression on both counts. Trajan, in the months of celebrations following his victories in Dacia in AD 107, sponsored ten thousand gladiatorial fights, as many as Augustus had provided in the whole of his forty-four year reign.

The level of entertainment provided by theatre and mime also suffered from the general degeneration in standards of taste. Plays became primarily vehicles for lavish spectacles; the appearance of 600 mules or whole squadrons of cavalry and infantry tended to steal the show and capture the applause. The mime, too, turned more and more towards sensationalism; at one performance in the reign of Domitian, a condemned criminal was substituted for an actor in the final scene so that the spectators might enjoy a real execution preceded by dreadful tortures.

There is, however, little reason to suppose that the more sensitive and discerning inhabitants of the city, in turning away from these degrading spectacles, and in protesting against the growth of moral laxity, sought an

Above: Temple of Isis, Pompeii, in a colonnaded court, now overgrown with grass.
Below: The market building at Pozzuoli.

alternative way of life through initiation into one of the mystery cults. For during the first century BC and even the first and second centuries AD, the initiates of the exotic Eastern cults at Rome and elsewhere in Italy were mostly to be found among immigrants and the lower social classes. With the exception of the cult of Cybele, which was patronized by the nobility at Rome and by prominent citizens at Ostia, wherever we have evidence from inscriptions of the names of the worshippers of the mystery cults, these names most often indicate people of foreign origin and humble status. It has been calculated that in southern Italy three-quarters of the dedicants in inscriptions to Isis are of non-Italian origin, and therefore were probably slaves or freedmen and women, while in Roman inscriptions to Isis the proportion of dedicants of non-Italian origin seems to have been about three-fifths. At Ostia, where a number of inscriptions recording the names of worshippers of Mithras has been found, the majority seem to have been of modest social standing, such as members of a ferry-boat or a builders' guild. No one who is known to have held public office at Ostia is found listed among the worshippers of Mithras there.

At Rome there was not apparently a significant number of converts to the mystery cults among the old ruling classes, the senators and knights, or the literary élite. Seneca, who came from a distinguished family of knights, was strongly opposed to the worship of Isis, while Suetonius regarded the cult as an empty superstition. Juvenal saw the Eastern cults as a sign of contemporary society's decadence. He mocks the enthusiasts for the cult of the Great Mother, who rush along in the train of a giant eunuch, to whom inferior priestlings do reverence, and he rails against the priest of Isis who, under the mask of Anubis, the dog-headed god, runs through the streets with his linen-clad and tonsured crew deriding the weeping crowds. Given the hostility of so many of the élite to the mystery cults, it is hardly surprising that the first emperors to wholly succumb to the oriental cults were the Flavians, Vespasian, Titus and Domitian, who came from a relatively poor and undistinguished family of tax-gatherers. Suetonius points out that Domitian spent a poverty-stricken and degraded youth, without even any silver on the family table.

Although the mystery religions might sometimes claim to be exclusive, they did not usually prosecute this claim with any great zeal. Despite the fact that the Eastern cults came from different countries originally – Cybele from Anatolia, Isis and Serapis from Egypt and Mithras from Iran – they are strikingly similar in their ideas about salvation and communion with the deity. The various deities of these cults are not impassive, but suffer or die and rise from the dead. The reason for their similarities seems to be that all these so-called oriental religions came to Italy after having been filtered through the sensibilities and mental attitudes of the Hellenistic world. Hence the common hue with which they are all tinged, the adaptation of their individual myths to the idea of a universal deity, and their common interest in astrology. Although each of these cults promised salvation to its initiates, in practice people were often initiated into more than one cult. The writer Apuleius recounts that he was initiated into several mystery cults, while a funerary inscription from Ostia commemorates a certain L. Valerius Fyrmus who was a priest of both Isis and Cybele. Moreover, worshippers often set up images or dedications to one god in the sanctuary of another.

The details of the rites and initiation ceremonies of the mystery religions are now rather obscure to us as these cults were secret societies; their mysteries were revealed only to their initiates. On the whole their secrets have been remarkably well kept, so that any account of these cults is bound to be fairly tenuous and problematic. The famous Eleusinian Mysteries celebrated at Eleusis in Greece may be considered first, as these were apparently the oldest mysteries celebrated in the classical world, going back beyond the seventh century BC, at which time Eleusis became an Athenian possession, and the Athenian state took charge of the cult. The prestige of the Eleusinian mysteries lasted right down to the end of the

pagan period, and it appears probable that the forms of worship of this famous cult influenced some of the rites which were later practised in the celebration of the oriental cults in Rome and Italy. It has been argued that the other mystery religions took over and incorporated important features of the Eleusinian cult, such as the institution of ceremonies of initiation. The Eleusinian cult was never transferred from Greece to Italy, although the emperor Claudius is said to have tried to do so. However, numerous prominent Romans, including Augustus and Marcus Aurelius, went to Eleusis to be initiated into the mysteries; this fact is symptomatic of the eclectic approach to religion taken by the pious Roman. Both Cicero and his friend Atticus, who were great admirers of Greek culture, were initiates of the Eleusinian Mysteries. In one of his *Dialogues* Cicero writes, 'Athens has plainly made many outstanding contributions to human life – gifts from heaven – but none better than those Mysteries. . . . The ceremonies are called initiations, and we recognize in them the first principles of living. We have gained from them the way of living in happiness and dying with a better hope' (*Laws*, II, 14, 36).

The Eleusinian Mysteries were celebrated in honour of Demeter the corn-goddess and Persephone the corn-maiden; in origin they were an agrarian cult and went back to very early times. The ritual concerned the death and rebirth of the corn, and, with the passing of time, hopes of rebirth and immortality for initiates came to be associated with it. The rites were celebrated in the Great Hall of the Mysteries at Eleusis, beginning in the evening and illuminated by torchlight. The secret of these mysteries has been well kept, so that although there has been much speculation we do not know exactly what the rites were. Very probably the story of Demeter and Persephone was dramatically represented, showing the rape of Persephone by Pluto, god of the underworld, and the mourning of her mother, Demeter, who refused to let the corn grow on earth until Persephone was reunited with her on earth for at least part of every year. The final stage of initiation consisted in the revealing of the sacred objects of the cult in a great blaze of light.

The Mysteries of Dionysus or Bacchus, also Greek in origin, gained numerous adherents in the Roman world. These rites were frequently celebrated in Rome and elsewhere in Italy, although no special buildings for the celebration of the Dionysiac Mysteries have been certainly identified. There were many members of this sect in southern Italy and Etruria in the early second century BC, and in 186 BC there was an outbreak of Bacchic frenzy in Rome which the Senate took official measures to combat, both because it was a secret society and because it promoted lawless and licentious behaviour. Certainly the celebration of the Dionysiac Mysteries seems frequently to have taken place amid frenzied dancing and drinking. Since Dionysus, who was assimilated with Bacchus in the Roman world, was a god of fertility and wine, it is hardly surprising that the mysteries connected with him assumed from time to time an orgiastic character. The cult of the Dionysiac Mysteries was chiefly, and perhaps exclusively, reserved for women – after all the ecstatic Maenads were the traditional followers of Dionysus.

The cult of Cybele, the Great Mother, did not simply infiltrate the population of Rome over a period of time. It was imported from Pessinus in Phrygia to Rome in 209 BC on the recommendation of the Sybilline Books, when the Romans were hard pressed in the Punic Wars. The great black stone, fetish of Cybele, was brought from Pessinus to Rome; it was formally met at the harbour by a religious procession in which women had unusual prominence. The stone was carried into the heart of the city, to the Palatine hill, where a magnificent temple was built to Cybele and dedicated in 191 BC. This temple was restored under Augustus. Even after the removal of the black stone to Rome, Pessinus remained an important centre of the cult, and we hear of prominent Romans, such as the general Marius, making pilgrimages to the sanctuary of Pessinus. In fact many of the Roman nobility were particularly attached to this cult.

Opposite : The amphitheatre at Pozzuoli, which dates from the first century AD, and is one of the largest and best preserved Roman amphitheatres. Amphitheatres were used for gladiatorial fights and for wild beast shows. Mock hunts of ferocious animals, many of them imported from Africa, were a popular spectacle. Condemned criminals, both male and female, were also thrown to the wild beasts in amphitheatres.

Below : Painting of a lion hunt which comes from the cemetery of Isola Sacra near Ostia.

Above : Model of a scaenae frons, or stage building, of a theatre. In the centre there is the so-called porta regia, (main entrance) onto the stage, and on each side the so-called hospitalia (secondary entrances). This model was perhaps a votive relief offered to the god Dionysus by a successful actor.

Cybele was a nature and fertility goddess, hence her cult was orgiastic. She was attended by eunuch priests who had castrated themselves in ecstasy during their initiation into her service. Attis, the youthful consort of Cybele, who is sometimes represented with the goddess in her chariot, was the prototype of the eunuch priests, for the high priest at Pessinus, and later the other priests also, took the name Attis. There are many variants of the myth about Cybele and Attis, but a common feature of them all is the self-castration of Attis. According to one account Attis had been abandoned as a baby by his mother, but was rescued by the goddess Cybele. He grew up into a beautiful youth, and Cybele fell in love with him. He was unfaithful to her, so she drove him mad. He castrated himself under a pine tree, and there he bled to death. In some versions of the myth, he rose to life again, so it has been conjectured that he was in origin a vegetation god.

Under the Republic the outlandish rites of worship for the goddess were largely confined in Rome to the temple precincts, and for the most part she was attended by eunuch priests imported from Phrygia, although occasionally Romans may have become her priests. Undoubtedly there was in Rome a strange fascination and revulsion felt by people with regard to the worship of Cybele by her eunuch priests; the poet Catullus, writing towards the end of the Republican period, powerfully evokes the reactions of a newly initiated priest of the cult – first his frantic ecstasy, and then his horror and revulsion. The story of Attis and Cybele was celebrated each year by a festival held in Rome. The festival began on 15 March with a procession of reed-bearers, who perhaps commemorated the discovery of the baby Attis among the reeds where he had been abandoned. Then came nine days of fasting and sexual abstinence during which, on 22 March, there was a procession of the tree-bearers, the devotees of the cult carrying uprooted pine trees to the temple in memory of the death of Attis. This was followed by the 'Day of Blood', a day of deep mourning when people lacerated themselves with knives, and when the new priests perhaps castrated themselves. The following day, 25 March, the period of fasting was over and the Hilaria, or festival of joy, was celebrated, commemorating, as a later writer tells us, the triumph of day over night after the spring equinox. After this, the celebrations were concluded with the 'Ceremony of Washing', in which the cult object was carried in a chariot accompanied by a procession to a river and washed; it was this soaking of the 'earth' in the rain which was believed to promote fertility. The emperor Claudius authorized these ceremonies to be performed in public, so that the festival became part of the official calendar, and the priesthood was officially opened to Roman citizens.

The sacrifice of a bull, called a *taurobolium*, was not originally part of the worship offered to Cybele, but some time in the second century AD sacrifices of this type appear to have been added to the cult. Records of such sacrifices offered by the devotees of Cybele on behalf of the reigning emperor and his family have been found at Ostia in the large sanctuary area of the Great Mother and her associates. Bulls might also be sacrificed for individuals, in which case the person concerned stood in a trench that had been dug for this purpose, and which was then covered by a board pierced by holes. The bull was sacrificed on the board so that its blood ran down and flowed through the holes into the pit below, completely covering the person seeking initiation. This baptism in bull's blood was thought to transfer the power of the bull to the initiate, and to purify him so that he was reborn to a new life, but in this world rather than the next. Some people repeated this ceremony after twenty years, and there are records of both women and men undergoing the initiation. There was also a sacramental meal associated with the cult which Christian writers were later to take as a demonic parody of the Eucharist.

Initiation into the cult of Mithras was gained only after the undergoing of considerable ordeals. This was a cult from which women were barred, and which appealed particularly to soldiers; it was Persian in origin, but through contact with Mesopotamia it assimilated a strong astrological

background. During the Hellenistic period this cult spread widely in Asia Minor, and it was said by Plutarch to have been brought to the West by the Cilician pirates whom Pompey later exterminated; if this was so, the cult must have been very much confined to the lowest classes living in the great ports of Italy, among whom in fact it flourished for a long time. Mithraism was popular over a long period: it appears first to have become much practised under the Flavians, and the cult was still widespread in the fourth century AD, by which time Mithras had been identified with the Invincible Sun god. From the middle of the first century AD onwards worship of Mithras spread with the occupying forces of the Roman armies, up the Danube and down the Rhone and the Rhine, and as far afield as Britain, where a Mithraeum was found in Walbrook in the City of London.

Mithras was usually worshipped in a small sanctuary constructed to look like the underground cave in which, according to tradition, he had been born. There were seven grades of initiates, each of which was associated with one of the planets. The lower grades, known together as Servitors, were Raven, Bridegroom, and Soldier, while the upper grades called collectively Participants, were Lion, Persian, Courier of the Sun, and Father. The ordeals the initiates had first to undergo might be of great severity, for in addition to fasting there were ordeals by scourging, branding, and exposure to extreme heat and cold, and they may sometimes have involved human sacrifice. A magical papyrus from Egypt of the early third century AD seems to preserve part of the liturgy for initiation into the highest grade of the cult, which consists of invocations and prayers for a spiritual rebirth.

In the unending war of good against evil Mithras was a good spirit, an attendant on Ahuramazda, the Lord of Life. He was also regarded as an agent of the Invincible Sun, with whom he was later identified. In fact he is sometimes shown, wearing the characteristic Phrygian cap, in the company of the Sun. Mithras's most important exploit was believed to have been the killing of a great bull, the first of living creatures, from whose blood sprang corn and all other life. Ahriman, the power of darkness, sent plagues and flames to try to overwhelm this new life, but Mithras overcame them, and so, having accomplished his mission on earth, he ascended to heaven in the chariot of the Sun. However, before the ascent to heaven Mithras and the Sun shared a sacred meal, which was afterwards re-enacted periodically by the followers of Mithras; it has been conjectured that initiates with the rank of Courier of the Sun and Father presided at these feasts, or communion services, as they have been called. It is hardly surprising that Christian

Frescoes decorating the Villa of the Mysteries, Pompeii, built in the second century BC. The frescoes date from the mid-first century BC. A mixture of human and divine or allegorical figures, they are suffused with Dionysiac imagery. Above: Fresco of an elaborately decorated doorway. Opposite: The Dancing Faun, in one of the bedrooms. Below: Apparently the initiation of a young woman into the Dionysiac Mysteries. Below right: A young satyr plays the pipes, his companion suckles a goat.

Left : Head of the mother-goddess Cybele, whose worship was imported to Rome from Phrygia in Asia Minor in the second century BC. She is wearing her characteristic high head-dress, or polos.

Above right : Third-century Mithraeum beneath the Church of S. Clemente, Rome. This underground sanctuary is one of the forty-five shrines dedicated to the worship of Mithras which have been found in Rome. It was originally lit from the top by light-wells designed to illuminate the Mithraic statues and the long benches down the sides of the sanctuary where the initiates sat in outlandish costumes appropriate to their rank. The vaulted ceiling was covered in pumice and mosaic to enhance the impression of its being a cave or grotto.

Right : The altar in the shrine.

Above : Small marble statue of Mithras, wearing the Phyrigian cap, in the Mithraeum.

Left : A relief of Mithras slaying the bull, the first of living creatures, from whose blood corn and all other forms of life arose. Traces of the original colouring can be seen.

writers took these feasts, as well, as parodies of the Eucharist.

The cult of the Egyptian goddess Isis, who was often worshipped together with the Egyptian gods, Serapis, Osiris and Harpocrates, was another very popular mystery religion in the Roman world. The worship of Isis and her associates was well established in Italy by the first century BC, especially in Campania, which had close links with Egypt. In spite of some setbacks and opposition to the cult, it appears to have gained ground, until in the later first century AD it was given added support by the patronage of the Flavian emperors; Vespasian's miracles at Alexandria were reportedly aided by the Egyptian gods. The worship of Isis seems to have been powerfully influenced by ideas of syncretism, that is, the conception that all human perceptions of the divine are really manifestations of one universal deity; Isis became identified with nearly every goddess of the known world, so that she came to be called 'Goddess of Ten Thousand Names', 'Star of the Sea' and 'Lady of All'. Isis was known as 'Glory of Women', for she was believed to have given women equal power with men; in one hymn she proclaims, 'I am she whom women call goddess. I ordained that women shall be loved by men; I brought wife and husband together, and invented the marriage contract'.

The worship of the goddess Isis and her associates was strongly institutionalized; the temples had a hierarchy of priests, and magnificent processions were organized in which the image of the goddess was carried,

Above : Domus Clementis, Rome, a private house of the late first century AD which has been excavated beneath the lower Church of S. Clemente. According to Christian tradition this was the house of St. Clement, martyred in AD 97. One of the rooms of this house was converted into a Mithraeum in the third century.

Right : Inscription with a dedication to the rural god Silvanus in a Roman wall under the Church of S. Clemente in Rome. The inscription records that the dedication was made as the result of a vision – probably one vouchsafed in sleep.

accompanied by music. The worshippers gained admission to the cult by a process of initiation, during which, after a period of fasting, the initiate was shown the universe and the gods of the underworld and those of the upper air in some kind of dramatic representation. The experience of initiation was understood as a form of spiritual rebirth, involving an intense emotional experience. The writer Apuleius, who underwent this initiation, gives an account of it in the *Metamorphoses*, in which Lucius's prayer powerfully evokes his devotion to Isis:

> Holy goddess, everlasting Saviour of mankind, ever generous in your help to mortals, you show a mother's warm love for the misfortunes of those in distress. No day passes, no night without a gracious act of yours. You protect men by land and sea. You lull the storms of life and stretch out your hand to rescue mortals. You can unravel the inextricably tangled web of Fate. . . . My ability is too scanty to praise you properly, my resources too scanty to honour you with sacrifice. But poor as I am I have taken a vow of devotion and shall be dutiful in doing all that I can. I shall always guard the picture of your divine features and your holy divinity in the sacred places of my heart.

Although the period when Christianity rose to ascendancy in the Roman world lies outside the scope of this book, it is perhaps worth pointing out that the cult of Isis, and to a lesser extent of some of the other mystery cults, have a number of features in common with Christianity. For the worship of Isis involved the whole personality, and demanded moral as well as ritual purity from those initiated into its mysteries. Moreover it provided for a spiritual rebirth and offered hope of a new start in life. It was a religion which was specially chosen by its Roman devotees; it was not confined to a particular nationality or class. Indeed like Christianity, it appears to have been specially welcoming to women and to slaves. The cult of Mithras also had points of similarity with Christianity; there was a similar sacred meal and the miraculous birth of the divine child, and initiation appears to have offered the hope of life after death, which was also a feature of some of the other mystery cults. So it was to a considerable extent owing to the mystery religions that a spiritual climate in tune with, and favourable to, the growth of Christianity began to grow up in the Roman world. Nevertheless, the eventual triumph of Christianity should not lead us to underestimate the strengths and importance of the traditional religious way of life of Rome. These traditional attitudes and beliefs had, after all, proved sufficiently adaptable and innovative to provide Roman society with strength, stability, and direction for a period of almost a thousand years.

Left : Tragic mask from the Villa of Mysteries, Pompeii. One of the rooms of this villa was redecorated in the late first century AD with a series of elegant frescoes with black backgrounds, chiefly showing Egyptian motifs and garden scenes. Above : Ibises. Right : A sacred winged serpent from Egypt. Below : Two Egyptian goddesses, perhaps Isis and Neftis, flanking a sacred crocodile. The inclusion of Egyptianizing motifs may indicate that the man who owned the villa at that time was a devotee of the Egyptian gods, or it may just reflect the contemporary vogue for Egyptian décor.

ACKNOWLEDGMENTS

Werner Forman and the publishers would like to acknowledge the help of the following museums in permitting the photography shown on these pages:
Antiquario Palatino, Rome: 31 below left and right, 62, 117 above; Auckland Institute and Museum, Auckland: 16 below; Museo Barracco, Rome: 12 below; British Museum, London: 30 above, 38, 39 above, 62 right, 66 above, 67, 98 above; Musei Capitolini, Rome: 12 above; J. Paul Getty Museum, Malibu: 2, 4, 44 top and above, 59, 81 above, 103, 105; Museo Gregoriano Profano, The Vatican, Rome: 9, 44 right, 101 above, 102, 116 above left; Museo Nazionale Romano, Rome: 1, 34, 83, 87, 90, 91, 98 left, 106, 107, 109, 111, 115 below, 120 above and below; Scavi di Ostia: 13 below, 22, 33 below, 39, 45, 86, 115 above.

Werner Forman would also like to thank the following for their assistance:
Ajša Bečková, Rome; Alessandro Califano, Rome; Serarcangeli Gianfranco, Rome; Linda Graham, Rome; Pietro Giovanni Guzzo, Rome; Jan Kosinka, Rome; Father Paul Lawlor, Rome; Fausta Manera, Rome; Mrs. Sapelli, Rome; Professor Surina, Rome; Dr. Vecchio, Naples.

SUGGESTIONS FOR FURTHER READING

Bandinelli, R. Bianchi *Rome : the Centre of Power* (London 1970)
Ferguson, J. *Greek and Roman Religion* (London 1980)
Hopkins, M. K. *Conquerors and Slaves* (Cambridge 1978)
Liebeschuetz, J. H. W. G. *Continuity and Change in Roman Religion* (Oxford 1979)
MacMullen, R. *Paganism in the Roman Empire* (New Haven and London 1981)
Meiggs, R. *Roman Ostia* (Oxford 1973)
Ogilvie, R. M. *The Romans and their Gods* (London 1969)
Scullard, H. H. *Festivals and Ceremonies of the Roman Republic* (London 1981)
Ward-Perkins, J. and Claridge, A. *Pompeii AD 79* (Bristol 1976)
Wilkinson, L. P. *The Roman Experience* (London 1975)

INDEX

Numbers in italics refer to captions

Achaia, 14
Actium, battle of (31 BC), 15, 61, 62, 67, *30*
aediculae (miniature temples), 86
Aemilius Paullus, 42
Aeneas, 30, 85, *56*
Aetolians, 41
after-life, 104, 113, 115
Agnano, *53*
Agricola, Gnaeus Julius, 104
agricultural cults, 25, 26, 38, 46–7, 69, 89, 106, 115
Agrippa, 74
Ahriman, 118
Ahuramazda, 118
Albano, Mount, 33
Alexander of Abonoteichus, 92
Alexander the Great, 71, 78
Alexandria, 78, 121
Altar of Augustan Peace, 38, 40, 68, 69
Altar of Augustan Piety, 40
altars, 38, 40, 68, 69, 74, 77, 104, *41*, *43*, *45*, *120*
Ambarvalia, 47
Ammianus Marcellinus, 29
amphitheatres, 112, *11*, *109*, *115*
Amphitrite, *85*
amulets, 89, 95, *86*, *104*
Amulius, King, 12
Anatolia, 113
ancestors, 25, 33, 37, 44, 67, 85, 95, 100, 101, 102, 104, *35*, *81*, *84*
animals: entrails of as omens, 51, 55, 58; festivals for, 48–9; sacrificial, 38, 40, 43, 47, 86, 96, 106, 117, *43*, *86*
Antonine emperors, 111

Antoninus Pius, 74, 111, *77*; Temple of Antoninus and Faustina, *77*
Antony, Mark (Marcus Antonius), 15, 61, 71, 74, 77
Anubis, 113
Aphrodite, 42, *21*, *26*; *see also* Venus
Apollo, 29, 42, 66–7, 86, *59*, *62*; House of Apollo, Pompeii, 86; Temple of *Apollo in Circo*, 42, 66; Temple of Apollo on the Palatine, 29, 66, 67, *30*
'Apotheosis of Homer', *43*
Appian Way *see* Via Appia
Apulieus, Lucius, 86, 92, 113, *123*
Ara Pacis Augustae see Altar of Augustan Peace
Arabia, 15
Arch of Augustus, *77*
Arch of Titus, 9, *35*, *37*, *66*
Aricia, *111*
Arval Brethren, 47, 69
Asclepius, 92, 94
Asia Minor, 15, 61, 76, 89, 92, 94, 109, 118, *120*
assemblies and auspices, 55
Assembly of the People, 66
astrology, 21, 78, 113, 117
Attalus, King of Pergamon, 15
Atticus, Pomponius, 115
Attis, 109, 117
auguraculum, 55
augurs and augury, 22, 24, 51, 54, 55, 58–9, 96
Augustus, 15, 17, 29, 40, 47, 61, 64, 66–71, 74, 76–8, 86, 89, 92, 96, 98, 104, 111, *30*, *61*, *64*, *83*, *117*; Altar of Augustan Peace, 38, 40, 68, 69; Altar of Augustan Piety, 40; Arch of Augustus, *77*;

Forum of Augustus, 46, 66; Temple of Divus Augustus, 74; Temple of Rome and Augustus (Ancyra), 77
Aurelian (Lucius Domitius Aurelianus), 18
Aurelian Walls, 18, *6*, *17*
Aurelius (Marcus Aurelius Antoninus), 92, 96, 112, 115
Aventine hill, 12, 31, 51

Baalbek, 40
Bacchus *see* Dionysus
Bandusia, spring of, 31
Basilica Julia, *77*
baths, 17–18, 84, *16*
Baths of Caracalla, *16*
bird flight and call, divination by, 24, 37, 51, 55
birth, 83, 94–5, 96
Board of Fifteen Keepers of the Sibylline Books, 24, 58, 59
Bona Dea, 51
Britain, 15, 89, 118
Brown, P., 91
Brutus, Marcus Junius, 61, 71
burial, 44, 89, 101, 104, 106, *4*, *47*, *93*, *97*; *see also* funeral rites *and* tombs

Caelian hill, 12
Caesar, Gaius Julius, 15, 22, 29, 51, 61, 66–7, 70–1, 74, 76, 89, *35*, *66*; Forum of Caesar, 67, *35*; Temple of Divus Julius, 66, 70, 74, 77
calendar, 22, 26, 43–9, 51, 70, 95, 102, 106, 117
Caligula, 38, 74
Camillus, Marcus Furius, 29
Campus Martius, 67, 68, 75
Cannae, battle of (216 BC), 48
Canopus, Hadrian's Villa, *70*, *74*

Capitol, 7, 12, 22, 34, 40, 42, 49, 55, 59, 67
Capitoline hill, 12, 18, 26, 29, 43, 51, *12*, *30*
Capitolium, 109, *30*
Cappadocia, 15
Caracalla, Baths of, *16*
Carcopino, 111
Carmen Saeculare, 67
Carrhae, battle of (54 BC), 55
Carthage, 14, 47–8
caryatids, *70*, *74*
Cassius (Gaius Cassius Longinus), 61, 71, 110
Castel Sant'Angelo, *78*
Castor and Pollux, 29, 71, *8*, *31*
Cato the Elder (Marcus Porcius Cato), 12–13, 47, 58, 106
census, 47
'Ceremony of Washing', 117
Ceres, 26, 47, 106–7
Christianity, 9, 22, 33, 35, 37, 42, 51, 62, 71, 89, 104, 107, 110–11, 117, 118, 123
Cicero, Marcus Tullius, 8, 12, 21, 24, 26, 30, 35, 37, 51, 54, 55, 61, 70, 96, 104, 115
Circus Maximus, 48, 51
Claudius I, 15, 46, 115, 117, *25*
Cleopatra, 15, 61, 77
Clitumnus, 107
Cloaca Maxima, 12
Clodius, Publius (surnamed Pulcher), 51
coins, 74, 76, 111, *64*
College of Augurs, 55
College of Epulones, 22
colleges of priests, 22, 24, 47, 68–9
Colosseum, *11*
Compitalia, 77
Concord, Temple of, 30–1

Constantine I (the Great), 7
consuls, 43–4, 49, 54, 69
Consus, 48
Corinth, 14
Crassus, Marcus Licinius, 48, 55
cremation, 101, 104, 106, 97
Cronus, 51
crossroads, spirits of the, 31, 77
cult statues, 40–42, 67, 70, 71, 74, 33
Cuma and the Cumaean Sibyl, 59, 54, 56, 58
curses, 86, 89, 92
Cybele (Magna Mater), 24, 59, 109, 110, 111, 113, 115, 117, 59, 120; Temple of Cybele, 66, 109, 115, 59

Dacia, victories in (AD 107), 15, 112, 15, 66
Dalmatia, 61
Dance of the Salii, 45
'Day of Blood', 117
Dea Dia, 69
death, 71, 83, 94, 98, 100–102, 104, 106; see also burial; cremation; funeral rites and tombs
decadence, 111–12
Decius, 106
deification: of emperors, 21, 66, 70–1, 74–8, 81, 77; of heroes, 24, 71, 92
Delos, 67, 77
Delphi, 29, 67
Delphic tripod, 30
Demeter, 115; see also Ceres
demons, 92
Diana, 42, 106, 30
dignitas, 33–4
Dion Cassius, 74
Dionysus (Bacchus), 95, 109, 110, 115, 45, 91, 117, 118
divination, 24, 37, 51, 54–5, 58–9, 83
divorce, 96
Domitian, 112, 113, 81; Stadium of Domitian, 19
drama, 112, 44, 117, 124
dreams, 92
Druids, 48, 110

Egypt, 61, 70, 91, 109, 111, 113, 118, 121, 123, 4, 15, 44, 64, 70, 81, 110, 111, 124
Eleusinian Mysteries, 111, 113, 115
Eleusis, 113, 115
emperors: deification of, 21, 66, 70–71, 74–8, 81, 77; events in honour of, 38, 39, 69, 74, 76, 111
entrails as omens, 51, 55, 58
Epulones, College of, 22
Erectheum, 70, 74
Esquiline hill, 12
Etruria, 13, 115
Etruscans, 12, 25, 29, 51, 58, 12
eunuchs, 117
Euryaces, Vergilius, 101

Fabius Maximus, 42
family and religion, 8, 9, 25, 26, 33–4, 35, 38, 44, 77, 83–7, 94–8, 100–102, 104, 106
Faunus, 44
Faustina, 96, 111, 77; Temple of Antoninus and Faustina, 77
'Fayum portraits', 104
fertility, 44, 46–7, 51, 89, 95, 96, 115, 117, 84, 87
festivals and feasts, 9, 22, 26, 29–30, 31, 37, 38, 40, 42–9, 51, 74, 77, 95–6, 102, 106, 117
Figulus, P. Nigidius, 91
figurines for magic purposes, 89, 91
Flavian emperors, 113, 118, 121, 9, 19
Flavian Palace, 81
Flora, 26, 47
Fors Fortuna, 48
Forum Boarium, 12, 29, 48
Forum Holitorium, 12
Forum of Augustus, 46, 66
Forum Romanum see Roman Forum
Fountain of Juturna, 29
freedmen and freedwomen, 21, 77, 84, 104, 106, 113, 49, 98
Fulvius, Marcus, 41
funeral rites, 71, 75, 98, 100–102, 104, 106, 15, 66, 86, 101
funerary portraits, 4, 15, 102, 104
Furrina, 9
Fyrmus, L. Valerius, 113

games, 22, 30, 40, 42–3, 47, 48, 49–51, 69, 71, 74, 76, 84, 104; 44, 109
Gaul and the Gauls, 13, 15, 40, 42, 48, 68
Gaza, 42
geese, sacred, 12
Genius, 77, 85, 86, 84
Germanicus Caesar, 87, 89
ghosts, 80, 95, 102
Gibbon, Edward, 7, 25
gladiators, 112, 11, 109, 114
Goethe, Johann Wolfgang von, 7, 48–9
government of Rome, 7–8, 12–13, 22, 35, 61, 66
Gracchi, 71, 74
Great Hall of the Mysteries, Eleusis, 115
Great Ludovisi Sarcophagus, 106
Great Mother see Cybele
Greece, 14–15, 25, 29–30, 33, 41–2, 54, 59, 67, 70, 71, 74, 77, 87, 89, 91, 92, 104, 109, 112, 113, 115, 21, 30, 33, 43, 45, 70, 74, 76
guild houses, 109

Hadrian, 74, 61, 66, 77; Hadrian's Villa, 26, 66, 69, 70, 74, 76; Mausoleum of Hadrian, 78
Halicarnassus, 76
Hannibal, 38, 42, 48, 59
Harpocrates, 121
haruspices (soothsayers), 55, 58–9, 83, 106
Haterii family tomb, 9, 101, 102
hearth cult, 26, 85, 51
Hecate, 89, 91
Herculaneum, 85–6, 85, 88
Hercules, 24, 29, 41, 48, 71, 78, 96, 111, 22, 30, 33, 44; Temple of Hercules, 109, 33
Herodian, 74–5
Hilaria, 117
'Homer, Apotheosis of', 43
Honos, shrines to, 31, 54
Horace, 15, 31, 33, 61, 64, 67, 89, 91, 98, 104
Horus, 102, 110
Hostilian, 106
House of Apollo, Pompeii, 86
House of the Menander, Pompeii, 84
House of Mosaic of Neptune and Amphitrite, 85
House of the Vestal Virgins, 26, 28, 51
House of the Vetii, Pompeii, 84
household gods, 25, 38, 77, 84–6, 95, 109, 111, 84
housing in Rome, 15, 17
human sacrifice, 47–8, 91, 118

illness, miracle cures for, 89, 92, 94
Illyricum, 61
immigrants, 15, 109–10, 113, 98
initiation ceremonies, 109, 113, 115, 117, 123, 118
Iran, 109, 113, 118
Iron Age village, Palatine hill, 12, 26
Isis, 109, 111, 113, 121, 123, 4, 9, 81, 102, 111, 124; Temple of Isis, Pompeii, 112
Isola Sacra cemetery, 25, 94, 96, 99, 101

Janiculum hill, 91
Janus, 26
Jerusalem, 41, 35
Judaism and the Jews, 37, 41, 91, 110, 111
Julian family, 35
Juno, 24, 25, 29, 49, 30; Juno Lucina, 95; Temple of Juno Moneta, 12
Jupiter, 22, 24, 26, 29, 34, 38, 42, 49, 66, 106, 109, 111, 30; Sanctuary of Jupiter Heliopolitanus, 40; Temple of Jupiter Optimus Maximus (Capitolinus), 7, 18, 22, 26, 29, 42, 43–4, 49, 59, 67, 30; see also Zeus
Juturna, Fountain of, 29
Juvenal, 17, 110, 113

'Lansdowne Throne', 59
Lares and Penates, 77, 84–6
Lares Augusti, 77
Lares compitales, 31, 77
Lateran Basilica, 18
Latin Festival, 33
Laurentum, 51
lectisternium (a ritual), 59
Lemuria, 95, 102, 104
Lepidus, 61, 77
Leto, 42
Liber Pater, 95
Livia, 40, 74, 83
Livy (Titus Livius), 29, 31, 33, 59, 62
Lucian, 38, 92
Lucina, 95, 98
Lucretius, 21
Ludi Romani, 49
Ludi saeculares, 67, 98
Lupercalia, 9, 44
lustratio, 47
lustrum, 47

Macedonia, 14, 42
Maecenas, Gaius Cilnius, 104
Maenads, 115, 117
magic, 78, 86–7, 89, 91–2, 94
magistrates, 22, 24, 38, 40, 48, 49, 51, 55, 59, 44
Manes (spirits of the dead), 44
Marcellus, Marcus Claudius, 41, 54
Marius, Gaius, 115
Markets of Trajan, 15
marriage, 44, 83, 84, 94, 95–6, 98, 121
Mars, 30, 38, 45–6, 47, 66, 67, 74, 106, 109, 111, 98; Campus Martius, 67, 68, 75; Temple of Mars Ultor, 46, 66, 67–8
Martial, 17, 106
Mauretania, 15
Mausoleum of Hadrian, 78
Menander, 117
Mercury, 86
Miletos, 77
Minerva, 29, 49, 30
Mithraea, 109, 118
Mithras, 109, 111, 113, 117–18, 120
mola salsa, 26, 48
morality and religion, 33–5, 83, 98, 112–13, 123
Muses, 41, 42, 43
mystery religions, 33, 51, 94, 104, 109–13, 115, 117–18, 121, 123

Naples, 76
natural phenomena as omens, 51, 55, 58–9, 71
necromancy, 91
Neftis, 124
Neptune, 85
Nero, 18, 37, 110–11, 112
North Africa, 14, 89, 92
Numa Pompilius, 26, 37
numina (spirits), 31, 106
Nymphs, 109

oaths, 34–5, 42, 71

Olympia, 42
Olympians, 30
omens, 21, 22, 24, 25, 37, 54–5, 58–9, 96
ordeals, 118
orgiastic rites, 109, 110, 115, 117, *117*
Oromasdes, 92
Orontes, River, 110
Osiris, 121, *102*
Ostia, 7, 9, 29, 96, 98, 101, 106, 109, 113, 117, *16, 22, 24, 25, 30, 33, 38, 41, 86, 94, 98, 117*
Ovid, 26, 31, 44, 46, 47, 48, 77, *102, 104*

Palatine hill, 12, 18, 29, 44, 66, 67, 115, *8, 19, 30, 81*
Pales, 46–7
Pan, *117*
Pantheon, 18, 74, *61, 66*
Parentalia, 44, 102
Parilia, 46
Parthians, 61
Paterculus, Marcus Velleius, 14, 66
paterfamilias, 83–4, 86
patrons and clients, 34
pax deorum ('peace of the gods'), 24, 98, 111
Penates *see* Lares and Penates
Pergamon, 15, 92, 94
Persephone, 115
Persia *see* Iran
Pessinus, 59, 115, 117
Petronius Arbiter, 84, 86, 104
Phidias, 42
Philippi, battle of (42 BC), 61, 67, 92
Philiscus, 42
Phrygia, 59, 115, 117, 118, *120*
Piazzale delle Corporazioni, *24, 117*
Pietas, 85; shrines to, 31
Piso, 87
Plebeian Games, 49, 51
Pliny the Elder, 8, 31, *88*
Pliny the Younger, 51, 104, 106–7
Plutarch, 38, 48, 71, 86, 118
Pluto, 89
poetry and religion, 30, 83, 89
politics and religion, 8, 22, 24, 55, 66, 69, 109, 112
Polybius, 35, 98, 100
Pomona, 26
Pompeia, 51
Pompeii, 7, 85–6, *84, 88, 93, 110, 112, 118, 124*
Pompey, 15, 40–41, 118
Pons Aelius, *78*
Pons Aemilius, *13*
Pons Sublicius, 48
pontifex maximus, 22, 26, 30, 44, 77
population of Rome, 15, 18
Porphyry, Bishop, 42
Porta Maggiore, *101*
Pozzuoli (Puteoli), 53, *56, 109, 115*
Priapus, 89, 91, *87*
priests, 12, 22, 24, 38, 40, 43,

44, 47, 48, 49, 64, 69, 117, 121; colleges of, 22, 24, 47, 68–9
Prima Porta, *83*
processions, 38, 40, 43, 45, 47, 48, 49, 51, 71, 96, 100, 117, *121*
puberty, 94, 95, *86*
Pudicitia, shrines to, 31
Pulcher, Appius Claudius, 91
Pulcher, Publius Claudius, 21, 55
Pulcher, Publius Clodius, *see* Clodius, Publius
Punic Wars, 14, 21, 55, 59, 115
Pyrrhus, King of Epirus, 13
Pythagoreanism, 91

Quindecimviri, 24, 58, 59
Quirinal hill, 12, *15*
Quirinus, *98*

Regia, 22, 26, 44
Regillus, battle of (498 BC), 29
Remus, 12, 44, *12*
Renaissance, 7
Rhodes, 77
ritual, correct performance of, 31, 33
rivers, cults of, 31
Robigus, 26, 38
Roma, 77
Roman Forum, 12, 18, 22, 26, 29, 40, 43, 48, 49, 51, 71, 74, 98, 100, *8, 9, 22, 31, 37, 51, 66, 77, 81*
Rome: great fire (AD 64), 18, 110, *28*; great plague (399 BC), 59; sack of (386 BC), 42
Rome and Augustus, Temple of (Ancyra), 77
Romulus, 12, 18, 37, 44, 55, 71, 78, *12*

Sabines, 13, 48
Sacraria Argeorum, 48
Sacred Way, 43, *9, 37*
sacrifices, 21, 29, 31, 33, 35, 37–8, 40, 42, 43, 44, 47–8, 49, 51, 58, 59, 67, 69, 71, 74, 83, 86, 89, 91, 95, 96, 100, 102, 104, 106, 111, 117, 118, *38, 43, 45, 84, 86*
St Antony, 48–9
St Augustine, 21, 84, 111
St Peter's, 18
Salii, 45–6, *98*
Samnites, 13
San Clemente, *97, 120*
Sanctuary dedicated to the Syrian gods, *91*
Sanctuary of Jupiter Heliopolitanus, 40
Sarculo, Antistius, *98*
Sardinia, 14
Saturn, 48, 51; Temple of Saturn, 51, 66
Saturnalia, 51
Scaevola, Mucius, 30
Scipio Aemilianus, 14
Scipio Africanus, 42, 66
Seleucia, 42
Senate, 12, 22, 40, 42, 44, 54,

59, 66, 70, 71, 77, 86, 95, 98, 110, 115, *77*
Seneca, Lucius Annaeus, 15, 17–18, 51, 96, 112, 113
Serapis, 78, 111, 113, 121, *81*
Severan emperors, 111
Sibylline Books, 24, 58, 59, 67, 69, 94, 115
Sibyls, *56*
Sicily, 14
Silenus, *45*
Silvanus, 106, 109
slaves, 14, 15, 21, 48, 51, 76, 77, 84, 86, 95, 101, 104, 106, 109, 110, 113, 123, *94, 98*
snakes, 67, 92, 94, *4, 59, 84*
society: and magic, 91–2; and religion, 22, 109, 113, 118
Spain, 14, 68
spirits, 31, 92, 102, 104, 106, *86*
Stadium of Domitian, *19*
statues, cult, 40–2, 67, 70, 71, 74, *33*
Stoa Poikile, Hadrian's Villa, *76*
Stoicism, 112
Storax, Lucius, 104
Subura, 67
Suetonius, 21, 37, 59, 66, 67, 70, 92, 113
Sulla, Lucius Cornelius, 48, 67, 86
Syracuse, 14, 41
Syria, 15

tabularium, 95
Tacitus, Cornelius, 24, 40, 59, 78, 81, 87, 104, 110, 111, 112
Tarentum, capture of (209 BC), 42
Tarquinius Priscus, 59
Teate, 104
Teatro Marittimo, Hadrian's Villa, *69*
Temple of Antoninus and Faustina, 77
Temple of *Apollo in Circo*, 29, 42, 66
Temple of Apollo on the Palatine, 29, 66, 67, *30*
Temple of Bona Dea, 51
Temple of Castor and Pollux, 29, *8, 31*
Temple of Concord, 30–1
Temple of Cybele, 66, 109, 116, *59*
Temple of Divus Augustus, 74
Temple of Divus Julius, 66, 70, 74, *77*
Temple of Hercules, 109, *33*
Temple of Isis, Pompeii, *112*
Temple of Juno Moneta, *12*
Temple of Mars Ultor, 46, 66, 67–8
Temple of Pales, 46
Temple of Rome and Augustus (Ancyra), 77
Temple of Saturn, 51, 66
Temple of Venus, Hadrian's Villa, *26*
Temple of Venus Genetrix, *35*

Temple of Vesta, 44, 48, *8, 22, 66*
Tertullus, 29
thanksgiving, 42, 69
theatre, 112, *44, 117, 124*
Thrace, 15
Tiber, River, 12, 17, 18, 25, 31, 48, 58, 67, 110, *13, 78*
Tiber Island, 12, 94
Tiberius, 15, 40, 58, 74, 87, 112, *31*
Tibullus, Albius, 18, 47
Tibur (Tivoli), 66, *69*
Tisiphone,, 91
Titus, 113, *9, 35, 37, 66*
Tomb of the Haterii, *9, 101, 102*
tombs, 83, 101–2, 104, *4, 9, 12, 22, 38, 44, 47, 49, 86, 88, 94, 96, 97, 98, 99, 101, 102, 106*
Trajan, 15, 112, *35, 67, 77*; Markets of Trajan, *15*; Trajan's Column, 67
Trasimene, Lake, 38
Trastevere, 18
Trevi (Trebiae), 107
Trimalchio, 84, 86, 104
Triumphs, 34, 41, 71, *35*
Twelve Tables, 83, 89, 102
Tyche, Naevoleia, *49*

Varro, Marcus Terentius, 9
Veii, 25, 29, 59
Venus, 29–30, 67, 74, 86; Temple of Venus, Hadrian's Villa, *26*; Temple of Venus Genetrix, *35*; Venus Genetrix, 67; *see also* Aphrodite
Vespasian, 21, 78, 81, 111, 113, 121, *11, 81*
Vesta and the Vestal Virgins, 26, 44, 47, 48, 51, 77, 85, 95, 96, *8, 22, 51*; House of the Vestal Virgins, 26, *28, 51*; Temple of Vesta, 44, 48, *22, 66*
Vesuvius, 85–6, *88*
Vetii, House of the, Pompeii, *84*
Via Appia, 102, *43, 47, 109*
vicomagistri (local leaders), 77
Villa Farnesina, *33*
Villa of the Mysteries, Pompeii, *110, 118, 124*
Viminal hill, 12
Virgil, 30, 47, 61, 64, 68, 71, 85, 91, 104, *56*
Virtus, shrines to, 31, 54
Voting Assemblies, 66

White Hen Villa, *83*
wild beast shows, 112, *115*
wolf, sacred, *12*

Zama, battle of (202 BC), 42
Zeus, 42, 51, *30, 43*; *see also* Jupiter
Zoroaster, 91, 92

128

DATE DUE

DEC 1 5 1994

GAYLORD

PRINTED IN U.S.A.

DATE DUE

DEC 1 5 1994